LOST SCROLLS

THE ANCIENT AND MEDIEVAL WORLD AT WAR

Written by Richard Bodley Scott and
Nik Gaukroger, assisted by James Hamilton,
Paul Robinson, Karsten Loh, Rudy Scott Nelson
and Richard Young

OSPREY
PUBLISHING

SLITHERINE

First published in Great Britain in 2010 by Osprey Publishing Ltd.

© 2010 Osprey Publishing Ltd and Slitherine Software UK Ltd.

Osprey Publishing, Midland House, West Way, Botley, Oxford OX2 0PH, UK
44–02 23rd St, Suite 219, Long Island City, NY 11101, USA
E-mail: info@ospreypublishing.com

Slitherine Software UK Ltd., The White Cottage, 8 West Hill Avenue, Epsom, KT 19 8LE, UK
E-mail: info@slitherine.co.uk

A CIP catalogue record for this book is available from the British Library

ISBN: 978 1 84908 158 0
E-book ISBN: 978 1 84908 159 7

Rules system by Richard Bodley Scott, Simon Hall and Terry Shaw
Page layout and cover concept by Myriam Bell Design, France
Index by Sandra Shotter
Typeset in Joanna Pro and Sleepy Hollow
Cover artwork by Peter Dennis
Photography by Irregular Miniatures, Venexia Miniatures, Old Glory UK, Mag
Aventine Miniatures, Khurasan Miniatures, Mirliton and Scotia Grendel
All artwork and cartography © Osprey Publishing Ltd
Project management by JD McNeil and Osprey Team
Technical management by Iain McNeil
Originated by PDQ Media, Bungay, UK
Printed in China through Worldprint Ltd

09 10 11 12 13   10 9 8 7 6 5 4 3 2 1

FOR A CATALOGUE OF ALL BOOKS PUBLISHED BY OSPREY MILITARY AND AVIATION
PLEASE CONTACT:

NORTH AMERICA
Osprey Direct, c/o Random House Distribution Center, 400 Hahn Road, Westminster, MD 21157
E-mail: uscustomerservice@ospreypublishing.com

ALL OTHER REGIONS
Osprey Direct, The Book Service Ltd, Distribution Centre, Colchester Road,
Frating Green, Colchester, Essex, CO7 7DW
E-mail: customerservice@ospreypublishing.com

FOR DETAILS OF ALL GAMES PUBLISHED BY SLITHERINE SOFTWARE UK LTD
E-mail: info@slitherine.co.uk

Osprey Publishing is supporting the Woodland Trust, the UK's leading woodland
conservation charity, by funding the dedication of trees.

www.ospreypublishing.com
www.slitherine.com

CONTENTS

INTRODUCTION

This book differs from the other Field of Glory Companions in not being based on a single historical and geographical theme. Instead it offers a mini-theme covering the early history of Rome, and a number of lists supplementing those covered by our other Field of Glory Companions.

THE SEVEN HILLS OF ROME

The "Seven Hills" theme covers the early wars of the Roman Republic, from the deposition of the monarchy and the attempt of Rome's Etruscan overlords to stamp on the fledgling Republic, through its epic struggles against its neighbours, till its eventual dominance of Italy.

In addition to the Romans themselves, these lists cover their sometimes enemies, sometimes allies the Latins, the enigmatic Etruscans, the fierce and resilient Samnites, the hill tribes of the Aequi, Aurunci, Hernici, Picentes, Sabines, Sidicini and Volsci, and the southern Italian Oscans of the Campanian plain, Apulia, Lucania and Bruttium. Together with the Gallic list in Field of Glory Companion 1: *Rise of Rome*, these lists form the "Seven Hills" theme. They can all also be used in tournaments based on the "Rise of Rome" theme.

THE LOST SCROLLS

The "Lost Scrolls" comprise a number of lists filling some gaps in the coverage of Ancient and Medieval warfare by our other Field of Glory Companions.

Firstly we include four lists from the earliest historical times, covering the armies of the nomadic and highland tribes surrounding the settled regions of Syria, Canaan and Mesopotamia, the early Elamites to the south-east of Mesopotamia, and the kingdoms the nomadic Amorites founded after their migration into the civilised areas. These armies are interesting in their own right, and will provide additional opponents for several of the armies in Field of Glory Companion 9: *Swifter than Eagles*.

Next, we have a list for Vietnamese armies of the Ancient and early Medieval period. This forms an addition to the lists covered by Field of Glory Companion 11: *Empires of the Dragon*.

Then, we provide four lists covering the settled and Bedouin armies of the Arabian peninsula prior to the ultimate victory of Islam, the Beja, Blemmye and Nobatian armies of the upper Nile valley and surrounding desert, and the Axumite kingdom of Abyssinia. These armies supplement those in Field of Glory Companion 5: *Legions Triumphant* and Field of Glory Companion 7: *Decline and Fall*.

Next, by popular demand, we include a list for those feared camel warriors, the Tuaregs of the Sahara.

Lastly, we include three supplementary lists for the "Storm of Arrows" theme, covering variant armies for which there was no space in Field of Glory Companion 2: *Storm of Arrows*. Two lists cover later medieval German city league and feudal armies in more detail than in the original volume. The *Storm of Arrows* Medieval German list should be used for Imperialist armies. The third list details the interestingly different armies of the Free Cantons of Frisia and Dithmarschen.

Camel enthusiasts will find much to please them in this book. Large numbers of camel warriors can be found in the Early Nomad, Beja, Nile Valley Blemmye and Early Nobatae and Tuareg lists, with lesser numbers in the Later Pre-Islamic Arabian and Later Pre-Islamic Bedouin lists.

EARLY REPUBLICAN ROMAN

This list covers Roman armies from the overthrow of the monarchy c.509 BC until 280 BC. It is part of the "Seven Hills" theme, and can also be used in themed tournaments based on Field of Glory Companion 1: *Rise of Rome*.

In Roman tradition, the city of Rome was founded in 753 BC. The Roman calendar counted years from this date — *ab urbe condita* (from the foundation of the city). Initially, Rome was ruled by kings, the last three of at least partly Etruscan origin. The final king, Tarquinius Superbus, was (according to tradition) overthrown in 509 BC and a republic formed.

There was an initial struggle to repel Etruscan attempts either to restore the monarchy or reduce the fledgling republic to vassal status, followed swiftly by a war to re-establish supremacy over Rome's Latin

Triarius

neighbours. Around 493 BC a mutual defence treaty was signed between Rome and the Latins against the mountain tribes.

In the early 4th century Rome conquered the Etruscan city of Veii to the north and subdued the Volsci to the south and the Aequi to the east. In 387 BC, however, Rome was sacked by an invading Gallic army under Brennos. The invaders were subsequently defeated and driven off by the Roman army under Marcus Furius Camillus.

After a short period of recovery from the damage done by the Gauls, the Romans once more began to expand. Over the course of the 4th century, they extended their hegemony into the territory of the Etruscans and Gauls to the north and the Samnites and Campanians to the south.

Following the First Samnite War (343–341 BC), a push by the Latins for equal status with Rome within the Latin League resulted in the Latin War (340–338 BC). It ended with the dissolution of the League, increased control by Rome, and the Latins being granted some rights and varying degrees of Roman citizenship.

By 280 BC, Rome controlled over half of the Italian peninsula.

TROOP NOTES

In the 6th and 5th centuries BC, Roman foot were divided into five classes. The first class, consisting of the wealthiest men, was required to muster with helmet, round hoplite shield, breastplate, greaves and long thrusting spear. The second class was required to have helmet, oval shield (*scutum*), greaves and spear. The third class, helmet, *scutum* and spear. The fourth class, according to Livy, was required to bring long thrusting spear and javelins only, but according to Dionysios of Halikarnassos, also a shield. The fifth class, according to Livy, was required to bring sling and stones only, but according to Dionysios, sling or javelins. The first class operated as a heavy hoplite phalanx, with the other classes in supporting roles. It is not known whether the first class formed up separately from the second and third classes, or whether it formed the front ranks of mixed bodies. The proportions of the different classes are also uncertain, as Livy specifies them in terms of centuries. If a standard sized century is assumed, the proportion of men qualifying for the first class (total property amounting to, or exceeding, 100,000 lbs weight of copper) seems implausibly high. As the Romans believed that greater property implied a greater stake in the state, and hence greater voting rights, it is likely that the first class was organised into smaller centuries than the lesser classes.

At some time in the 4th century BC, probably after the First Samnite War, the Roman army was extensively reformed. Thereafter, the legion no longer operated as a hoplite phalanx, instead being divided into more manoeuvrable sub-units called maniples, each of 120 men. These were deployed in a chequer-board formation, with the gaps between the maniples of the first "line" being covered by the maniples of the second "line". The heavy infantry of the legion formed

Roman Hoplites fleeing Celtic warriors, by Richard Hook. Taken from Men-At-Arms 283: Early Roman Armies.

up in three "lines". All used the large oval *scutum*. The front "line", the *hastati*, comprising the "flower of the young men", were armed with a new weapon, the *pilum* – a heavy throwing spear. In advance of these, light infantry called *leves* skirmished with javelins. The second heavy infantry "line", the *principes*, were the mainstay of the army, men in their prime, who, in this period, continued to use the thrusting spear as their weapon. The third "line", the *triarii*, comprised a smaller number of the older men, also armed with thrusting spears. Two additional classes of troops are recorded. The first of these is the *rorarii*, This may simply be another name for the *leves*,

Roman Musician

or they may have been light infantry attached to the *triarii*. The second is the *accensi*, who were the baggage attendants and only committed in an extreme emergency – they are only recorded as fighting on one occasion.

Battle groups of *hastati* and *principes* represent the maniples of the first and second heavy infantry "lines", deployed in manipular chequer-board formation. Although the *principes* were armed with long thrusting spears in this period, the overall effect of the formation is best represented under the rules by classification as Impact Foot, Swordsmen.

From the end of the Latin War in 338, Latin allies were organised into *alae* with the same infantry structure as Roman legions, but with more cavalry. From that date we do not distinguish them from Roman troops – they are included in the normal maxima for cavalry, *hastati* & *principes*, *triarii*, *leves*, *rorarii* and *accensi*.

EARLY REPUBLICAN ROMAN STARTER ARMY (405–341 BC)		
Commander-in-Chief	1	Field Commander
Sub-commanders	2	2 x Troop Commander
Cavalry	2 BGs	Each comprising 4 bases of cavalry: Average, Armoured, Undrilled Cavalry – Light Spear, Swordsmen
Separately deployed infantry of the 1st class	2 BGs	Each comprising 6 bases of infantry of the 1st class: Superior, Armoured, Drilled Heavy Foot – Offensive Spearmen
Separately deployed infantry of the 2nd or 3rd class	2 BGs	Each comprising 8 bases of infantry of the 2nd or 3rd class: Average, Protected, Drilled Heavy Foot – Offensive Spearmen
Infantry of the 4th class	2 BGs	Each comprising 6 bases of infantry of the 4th class: Average, Unprotected, Undrilled Light Foot – Javelins, Light Spear
Infantry of the 5th class	2 BGs	Each comprising 6 bases of infantry of the 5th class: Average, Unprotected, Undrilled Light Foot – Sling
Camp	1	Unfortified camp
Total	10 BGs	Camp, 8 mounted bases, 52 foot bases, 3 commanders

EARLY REPUBLICAN ROMAN STARTER ARMY (340–280 BC)		
Commander-in-Chief	1	Troop Commander
Sub-commanders	2	2 x Troop Commander
Cavalry	2 BGs	Each comprising 4 bases of cavalry: Average, Armoured, Undrilled Cavalry – Light Spear, Swordsmen
Hastati & Principes	6 BGs	Each comprising 4 bases of hastati & principes: Average, Armoured, Drilled Heavy Foot – Impact Foot, Swordsmen
Triarii	3 BGs	Each comprising 2 bases of triarii: Superior, Armoured, Drilled Heavy Foot – Offensive Spearmen
Leves	3 BGs	Each comprising 4 bases of leves: Average, Unprotected, Drilled Light Foot – Javelins, Light Spear
Accensi	1 BG	8 bases of accensi: Poor, Protected, Undrilled Heavy Foot – Defensive Spearmen
Camp	1	Unfortified camp
Total	15 BGs	Camp, 8 mounted bases, 50 foot bases, 3 commanders

BUILDING A CUSTOMISED LIST USING OUR ARMY POINTS

Choose an army based on the maxima and minima in the list below. The following special instructions apply to this army:

- Commanders should be depicted as cavalry.
- Before 340 BC cavalry can always dismount as Superior, Armoured or Protected (as mounted type), Undrilled, Heavy Foot, Impact Foot, Swordsmen.
- 1st class infantry must either all be deployed separately or all be deployed in mixed battle groups with 2nd and 3rd class infantry.
- If deployed separately, the army cannot include more battle groups of 1st class infantry than it includes of 2nd and 3rd class infantry.
- The minima marked * only apply if the Heavy Foot classes are deployed separately.
- The minimum marked ** only applies if mixed bodies of 1st, 2nd and 3rd class infantry are used.
- If any 1st, 2nd or 3rd class infantry are Drilled, all must be.

- Latin allied foot cannot be Drilled unless Roman 1st, 2nd and 3rd classes are.
- Hastati, principes and triarii must be organised as legions: Hastati and principes are brigaded together as battle groups. Depending on the size of army represented, a legion could be organised as 2 battle groups, each of 4 hastati & principes, and 1 battle group of 2 triarii, or as 2 battle groups, each of 8 hastati & principes, and 1 battle group of 4 triarii.
- It is recommended that each legion be deployed with its hastati & principes in front and its triarii in support behind.
- If part of a legion is upgraded, the whole legion must be upgraded.
- If part of a legion is downgraded, the whole legion including leves must be downgraded.
- The army, including allies, cannot include more than a total of 12 bases of cavalry.
- Only one non-Latin allied contingent can be used.

Cavalryman

EARLY REPUBLICAN ROMAN

Territory Types: Agricultural, Developed, Hilly

C-in-C	Inspired Commander/Field Commander/Troop Commander		80/50/35	1
Sub-commanders	Field Commander		50	0–2
	Troop Commander		35	0–3

Troop name		Troop Type				Capabilities		Points per base	Bases per BG	Total bases
		Type	Armour	Quality	Training	Shooting	Close Combat			
Core Troops										
Cavalry		Cavalry	Armoured	Average	Undrilled	–	Light Spear, Swordsmen	12	4–6	4–8
			Protected					9		
Separately deployed infantry of the 1st class	Only before 340	Heavy Foot	Armoured	Superior	Undrilled	–	Offensive Spearmen	12	6–8	*8–24
				Average				9		
	Only from 405 to 341	Heavy Foot	Armoured	Superior	Drilled	–	Offensive Spearmen	13	6–8	
				Average				10		
Separately deployed infantry of the 2nd or 3rd class	Only before 340	Heavy Foot	Protected	Average	Undrilled	–	Offensive Spearmen	7	6–8	*8–84
	Only from 405 to 341	Heavy Foot	Protected	Average	Drilled	–	Offensive Spearmen	8	6–8	
Mixed infantry of the 1st, 2nd and 3rd classes	Only before 340	Heavy Foot	Armoured	Average	Undrilled	–	Offensive Spearmen	9	6–8	0–32 / **20–116
	Only from 405 to 341	Heavy Foot	Armoured	Average	Drilled	–	Offensive Spearmen	10	6–8	
	Only before 340	Heavy Foot	Protected	Average	Undrilled	–	Offensive Spearmen	7	6–8	0–116
	Only from 405 to 341	Heavy Foot	Protected	Average	Drilled	–	Offensive Spearmen	8	6–8	
Infantry of the 4th class	Only before 340	Medium Foot	Protected	Average	Undrilled	–	Light Spear	5	6–8	6–24
			Unprotected					4		
		Light Foot	Unprotected	Average	Undrilled	Javelins	Light Spear	4	6–8	
Infantry of the 5th class		Light Foot	Unprotected	Average	Undrilled	Sling	–	4	6–8	6–16
				Poor				2		
		Light Foot	Unprotected	Average	Undrilled	Javelins	Light Spear	4	6–8	
				Poor				2		
Hastati and principes		Heavy Foot	Armoured	Average	Drilled	–	Impact Foot, Swordsmen	10	4–8	16–56
			Protected					8		
Triarii		Heavy Foot	Armoured	Superior	Drilled	–	Offensive Spearmen	13	2–4	1 per 4 hastati and principes
				Average				10		
Leves		Light Foot	Unprotected	Average	Drilled	Javelins	Light Spear	4	4–8	1 per 2 hastati and principes
Upgrade veteran legions to:	Only from 340	Heavy Foot	Armoured	Superior	Drilled	–	Impact Foot, Skilled Swordsmen	14	4–8	0–16
			Protected					11		
		Heavy Foot	Armoured	Elite	Drilled	–	Offensive Spearmen	16	2–4	1 per 4 hastati and principes
				Superior				13		
		Light Foot	Unprotected	Average	Drilled	Javelins	Light Foot	4	4–8	1 per 2 hastati and principes
Downgrade unenthusiastic allies or raw legions to:		Heavy Foot	Protected	Poor	Drilled	–	Impact Foot, Swordsmen	6	4–8	0–16
		Heavy Foot	Protected	Poor	Drilled	–	Offensive Spearmen	6	2–4	1 per 4 hastati & principes
		Light Foot	Unprotected	Poor	Drilled	Javelins	Light Foot	2	4–8	1 per 2 hastati and principes

Optional Troops									
Rorarii		Light Foot	Unprotected	Average	Drilled	Javelins	Light Spear	4	4–8	0–8
Accensi	Only from 340	Heavy Foot	Protected	Poor	Undrilled	–	Defensive Spearmen	4	6–8	0–8
Lighter equipped Italian allied infantry		Medium Foot	Protected	Average	Drilled	–	Light Spear, Swordsmen	7	6–8	0–12
				Poor				5		
Allies										
Campanian allies (Only from 343)										
Hernician allies (Only before 387) – Italian Hill Tribes										
Latin allies (Only before 340) – up to 2 contingents										
Lucanian allies (Only from 298 to 290)										
Samnite allies (Only in 340)										

EARLY REPUBLICAN ROMAN ALLIES

Allied commander		Field Commander/Troop Commander						40/25		1
Troop name		Troop Type				Capabilities		Points per base	Bases per BG	Total bases
		Type	Armour	Quality	Training	Shooting	Close Combat			
Cavalry		Cavalry	Armoured	Average	Undrilled	–	Light Spear, Swordsmen	12	4	0–4
			Protected					9		
Separately deployed infantry of the 1st class	Only before 340	Heavy Foot	Armoured	Superior	Undrilled	–	Offensive Spearmen	12	6–8	*6–8
				Average				9		
	Only from 405 to 341	Heavy Foot	Armoured	Superior	Drilled	–	Offensive Spearmen	13	6–8	
				Average				10		
Separately deployed infantry of the 2nd or 3rd class	Only before 340	Heavy Foot	Protected	Average	Undrilled	–	Offensive Spearmen	7	6–8	*6–16
	Only from 405 to 341	Heavy Foot	Protected	Average	Drilled	–	Offensive Spearmen	8	6–8	
Mixed infantry of the 1st, 2nd and 3rd classes	Only before 340	Heavy Foot	Armoured	Average	Undrilled	–	Offensive Spearmen	9	6–8	0–12
	Only from 405 to 341	Heavy Foot	Armoured	Average	Drilled	–	Offensive Spearmen	10	6–8	**8–24
	Only before 340	Heavy Foot	Protected	Average	Undrilled	–	Offensive Spearmen	7	6–8	0–24
	Only from 405 to 341	Heavy Foot	Protected	Average	Drilled	–	Offensive Spearmen	8	6–8	
Infantry of the 4th class	Only before 340	Medium Foot	Protected	Average	Undrilled	–	Light Spear	5	6–8	0–8
			Unprotected					4		
		Light Foot	Unprotected	Average	Undrilled	Javelins	Light Spear	4	6–8	
Infantry of the 5th class		Light Foot	Unprotected	Average	Undrilled	Sling	–	4	4–6	0–6
				Poor				2		
		Light Foot	Unprotected	Average	Undrilled	Javelins	Light Spear	4	4–6	
				Poor				2		

Hastati and principes		Heavy Foot	Armoured	Average	Drilled	—	Impact Foot, Swordsmen	10	4–8	8–24
			Protected					8		
Triarii		Heavy Foot	Armoured	Superior	Drilled	—	Offensive Spearmen	13	2–4	1 per 4 hastati and principes
				Average				10		
Leves		Light Foot	Unprotected	Average	Drilled	Javelins	Light Spear	4	4–8	1 per 2 hastati and principes
Upgrade veteran legions to:	Only from 340	Heavy Foot	Armoured	Superior	Drilled	—	Impact Foot, Skilled Swordsmen	14	4–8	0–8
			Protected					11		
		Heavy Foot	Armoured	Elite	Drilled	—	Offensive Spearmen	16	2–4	1 per 4 hastati and principes
				Superior				13		
		Light Foot	Unprotected	Average	Drilled	Javelins	Light Foot	4	4–8	1 per 2 hastati and principes
Downgrade unenthusiastic allies or raw legions to:		Heavy Foot	Protected	Poor	Drilled	—	Impact Foot, Swordsmen	6	4–8	0–8
		Heavy Foot	Protected	Poor	Drilled	—	Offensive Spearmen	6	2–4	1 per 4 hastati & principes
		Light Foot	Unprotected	Poor	Drilled	Javelins	Light Foot	2	4–8	1 per 2 hastati and principes

ETRUSCAN LEAGUE

This list covers the armies of the Etruscan League from its foundation in the early 7th century BC until final conquest by Rome in 280 BC. It is part of the "Seven Hills" theme, and can also be used in themed tournaments based on Field of Glory Companion 1: Rise of Rome.

The origin of the Etruscans is uncertain. They appear to have spoken a non-Indo-European language. They may have been native to Italy (pre-dating the influx of Indo-Europeans) or from outside — possibly even from Anatolia (modern Turkey). From a core territory in modern Tuscany, they expanded north into the Po valley and south into Latium (modern Lazio) and Campania.

Etruscan Officer

Historians do not agree on which cities comprised the twelve cities of the League, but the following are probable: Arretium (Arezzo), Caisra (Caere – modern Cerveteri), Clevsin (Clusium – modern Chiusi), Curtun (modern Cortona), Felathri (Volaterrae – modern Volterra), Perusna (Perugia), Pupluna (Populonia), Tarchna (Tarquinii – modern Tarquinia-Corneto), Veii, Velzna (Volsinii – modern Bolsena), Velch (Vulci – modern Volci) and Vetluna (Vetulonia). Once a year, according to Livy, representatives of the twelve cities met at the Fanum Voltumnae at Volsinii to choose a leader for the following year.

In the 6th century, the Etruscans allied themselves with Carthage against the Greek cities of southern Italy and Sicily (Magna Graecia). Around 540 BC, the joint fleets of the Etruscans and Carthaginians defeated a Phokaian fleet near the Phokaian colony of Alalia in Corsica (modern Aléria). Corsica was divided between the

Etruscan Hoplite (left), Latin Hoplite (right) and Horatius at the bridge, by Richard Hook. Taken from Men-At-Arms 283: Early Roman Armies.

Etruscans and Carthage, which also kept Sardinia. The Etruscans held control of the Tyrrhenian Sea.

Early Rome was dominated by the Etruscans, the last three kings being of at least partly Etruscan origin. Following the overthrow of the Roman monarchy in 509 BC, according to Livy, an attempt by the Etruscans, under Lars Porsena of Clevsin, to restore the deposed Roman king, Tarquinius Superbus, was unsuccessful. According to other ancient writers, however, Porsena did succeed in subjugating Rome for a time, but did not restore Tarquinius Superbus, and soon lost control again. In the following years Rome established its primacy in Latium.

In 480 BC the Carthaginians were defeated in Sicily by the Greeks led by Gelon, tyrant of Syracuse, and Theron, tyrant of Akragas (modern Agrigento). In 474 BC the combined fleets of Hieron I of Syracuse and Aristodemos of Cumae (a Greek city north-west of modern Naples) defeated the Etruscan fleet near Cumae. Following this, the Etruscans lost control of the Tyrrhenian Sea, and their decline began in earnest.

In the late 5th century BC the Etruscan cities in Campania were lost to the Oscan Campani. Around 400 BC, the Etruscan cities in the Po valley were lost to the Gauls, although Felsina (modern Bologna) held out till c.350. In 396 BC, Veii, one of the richest Etruscan cities, only 16 kilometres north-north-west of Rome, fell to the Romans. The surviving Etruscan cities subsequently fought several wars with Rome,

sometimes allied with the Samnites and/or Gauls. Around 282 BC, the Etruscans and their Gallic allies were decisively defeated by the Romans near Lake Vadimo. Thereafter Etruria came firmly under Roman control.

TROOP NOTES

Etruscan infantry were divided into a number of classes on the basis of wealth. The first class consisted of armoured hoplites with round hoplite shields and wielding a long thrusting spear. The second and third classes were armed with oval *scutum* and spear. It is not known whether the first class formed up separately from the second and third classes, or whether they formed up in mixed bodies. The fourth class was of skirmishers.

Rome, under heavy Etruscan influence, and ruled by Etruscan kings until 509, had an almost identical organisation until some time in the 4th century BC.

Devoted troops swore an oath to die rather than retreat. Some armoured troops in the early part of the period were armed with two-handed axes.

In the 4th century, some Etruscan infantry were re-equipped with the *pilum* – the heavy throwing spear adopted by the Romans. However, there is no evidence of division into separate lines like the Roman *hastati*, *principes* and *triarii*.

Etruscan Axeman

ETRUSCAN LEAGUE STARTER ARMY (405–331 BC)		
Commander-in-Chief	1	Troop Commander
Sub-commanders	2	2 x Troop Commander
Cavalry	2 BGs	Each comprising 4 bases of cavalry: Superior, Armoured, Undrilled Cavalry – Light Spear, Swordsmen
Devoted infantry	1 BG	4 bases of devoted infantry: Superior, Armoured, Drilled Heavy Foot – Offensive Spearmen
Separately deployed infantry of the 1st class	2 BGs	Each comprising 6 bases of infantry of the 1st class: Average, Armoured, Drilled Heavy Foot – Offensive Spearmen
Separately deployed infantry of the 2nd or 3rd class	2 BGs	Each comprising 8 bases of infantry of the 2nd or 3rd class: Average, Protected, Drilled Heavy Foot – Offensive Spearmen
Infantry of the 4th class	1 BG	6 bases of infantry of the 4th class: Average, Unprotected, Undrilled Light Foot – Javelins, Light Spear
Infantry of the 4th class	1 BG	8 bases of infantry of the 4th class: Poor, Unprotected, Undrilled Light Foot – Bow
Infantry of the 4th class	1 BG	8 bases of infantry of the 4th class: Poor, Unprotected, Undrilled Light Foot – Sling
Camp	1	Unfortified camp
Total	10 BGs	Camp, 8 mounted bases, 54 foot bases, 3 commanders

BUILDING A CUSTOMISED LIST USING OUR ARMY POINTS

Choose an army based on the maxima and minima in the list below. The following special instructions apply to this army:

- Commanders should be depicted as cavalry or infantry of the 1st class.
- 1st class infantry must either all be deployed separately or all be deployed in mixed battle groups with 2nd and 3rd class infantry.
- If deployed separately, the army cannot include more battle groups of 1st class infantry than it includes of 2nd and 3rd class infantry.

- The minima marked * only apply if the Heavy Foot classes are deployed separately.
- The minimum marked ** only applies if mixed bodies of 1st, 2nd and 3rd class infantry are used.
- Gallic, Samnite and Umbrian allies can be used together from 330, otherwise only one allied contingent can be used.

Etruscan 1st class Infantryman

ETRUSCAN LEAGUE

Territory Types: Agricultural, Developed, Hilly

Troop name		Troop Type				Capabilities		Points per base	Bases per BG	Total bases
		Type	Armour	Quality	Training	Shooting	Close Combat			
C-in-C		Inspired Commander/Field Commander/Troop Commander						80/50/35		1
Sub-commanders		Field Commander						50		0–2
		Troop Commander						35		0–3
Core Troops										
Cavalry		Cavalry	Armoured	Superior	Undrilled	–	Light Spear, Swordsmen	16	4–6	4–12
			Armoured	Average				12		
			Protected	Superior				12		
			Protected	Average				9		
Separately deployed infantry of the 1st class	Only before 330	Heavy Foot	Armoured	Average	Undrilled	–	Offensive Spearmen	9	6–8	*8–24
	Only from 405	Heavy Foot	Armoured	Average	Drilled	–	Offensive Spearmen	10	6–8	
Separately deployed infantry of the 2nd or 3rd class	Only before 330	Heavy Foot	Protected	Average	Undrilled	–	Offensive Spearmen	7	6–8	*8–80
				Poor				5		
	Only from 405	Heavy Foot	Protected	Average	Drilled	–	Offensive Spearmen	8	6–8	
				Poor				6		
	Only from 330	Heavy Foot	Protected	Average	Drilled	–	Impact Foot, Swordsmen	8	6–8	
				Poor				6		
Mixed infantry of the 1st, 2nd and 3rd classes	Only before 330	Heavy Foot	Armoured	Average	Undrilled	–	Offensive Spearmen	9	6–8	0–32 / **20–104
				Poor				7		
	Only from 405	Heavy Foot	Armoured	Average	Drilled	–	Offensive Spearmen	10	6–8	
				Poor				8		
	Only from 330	Heavy Foot	Armoured	Average	Drilled	–	Impact Foot, Swordsmen	10	6–8	
				Poor				8		
	Only before 330	Heavy Foot	Protected	Average	Undrilled	–	Offensive Spearmen	7	6–8	0–104
				Poor				5		
	Only from 405	Heavy Foot	Protected	Average	Drilled	–	Offensive Spearmen	8	6–8	
				Poor				6		
	Only from 330	Heavy Foot	Protected	Average	Drilled	–	Impact Foot, Swordsmen	8	6–8	
				Poor				6		
Infantry of the 4th class		Light Foot	Unprotected	Average	Undrilled	Bow	–	5	6–8	0–8	6–24
				Poor				3		
		Light Foot	Unprotected	Average	Undrilled	Sling	–	4	6–8	0–8
				Poor				2		
		Light Foot	Unprotected	Average	Undrilled	Javelins	Light Spear	4	6–8	6–24
				Poor				2		
Optional Troops										
Chariots	Only before 500	Light Chariots	–	Superior	Undrilled	–	Light Spear	15	4–6	0–6
Axemen	Only before 405	Heavy Foot	Armoured	Superior	Undrilled	–	Heavy Weapon	12	4	
Devoted foot	Only before 330	Heavy Foot	Armoured	Superior	Undrilled	–	Offensive Spearmen	12	4	0–4
	Only from 405	Heavy Foot	Armoured	Superior	Drilled	–	Offensive Spearmen	13	4	
Peasant levies		Mob	Unprotected	Poor	Undrilled	–	–	2	10–12	0–12
Allies										

Gallic allies – See Field of Glory Companion 1: *Rise of Rome*

Italiot allies – Classical Greek – See Field of Glory Companion 3: *Immortal Fire*

Latin allies (Only before 500)

Roman allies (Only from 506 to 501) – Early Republican Roman

Sabine allies – Italian Hill Tribes

Samnite allies

Umbrian allies

ETRUSCAN ALLIES

Troop name		Troop Type				Capabilities		Points per base	Bases per BG	Total bases
Allied commander		Field Commander/Troop Commander						40/25		1
		Type	Armour	Quality	Training	Shooting	Close Combat			
Cavalry		Cavalry	Armoured	Superior	Undrilled	—	Light Spear, Swordsmen	16	4	0–4
			Armoured	Average				12		
			Protected	Superior				12		
			Protected	Average				9		
Separately deployed infantry of the 1st class	Only before 330	Heavy Foot	Armoured	Average	Undrilled	—	Offensive Spearmen	9	6–8	*6–8
	Only from 405	Heavy Foot	Armoured	Average	Drilled	—	Offensive Spearmen	10	6–8	
Separately deployed infantry of the 2nd or 3rd class	Only before 330	Heavy Foot	Protected	Average	Undrilled	—	Offensive Spearmen	7	6–8	*6–24
				Poor				5		
	Only from 405	Heavy Foot	Protected	Average	Drilled	—	Offensive Spearmen	8	6–8	
				Poor				6		
	Only from 330	Heavy Foot	Protected	Average	Drilled	—	Impact Foot, Swordsmen	8	6–8	
				Poor				6		
Mixed infantry of the 1st, 2nd and 3rd classes	Only before 330	Heavy Foot	Armoured	Average	Undrilled	—	Offensive Spearmen	9	6–8	0–12 / **8–32
				Poor				7		
	Only from 405	Heavy Foot	Armoured	Average	Drilled	—	Offensive Spearmen	10	6–8	
				Poor				8		
	Only from 330	Heavy Foot	Armoured	Average	Drilled	—	Impact Foot, Swordsmen	10	6–8	
				Poor				8		
	Only before 330	Heavy Foot	Protected	Average	Undrilled	—	Offensive Spearmen	7	6–8	0–32
				Poor				5		
	Only from 405	Heavy Foot	Protected	Average	Drilled	—	Offensive Spearmen	8	6–8	
				Poor				6		
	Only from 330	Heavy Foot	Protected	Average	Drilled	—	Impact Foot, Swordsmen	8	6–8	
				Poor				6		
Infantry of the 4th class		Light Foot	Unprotected	Average	Undrilled	Javelins	Light Spear	4	6–8	0–8
				Poor				2		

UMBRIAN ALLIES

Umbrian Hoplite

Umbria is a region of central Italy, bordering on Tuscany to the north-west and Lazio to the south-west. Ancient Umbria thus bordered on the territories of the Etruscans and the Romans and Latins. Very little is known about the military system of the Umbrians, so this allies list is highly speculative. The late 5th century Mars of Todi depicts an armoured spearman and bears an inscription in Umbrian. This and other depictions suggest that they had some hoplites at least. The hilly and mountainous nature of the Umbrian terrain suggests that other foot would probably be best graded as Medium Foot.

The following special instructions apply to this allies list:

- Commanders should be depicted as cavalry.
- If any HF or MF are Drilled, all HF and MF must be Drilled.

UMBRIAN ALLIES

Allied commander		Field Commander/Troop Commander						40/25		1	
Troop name		Troop Type				Capabilities		Points per base	Bases per BG	Total bases	
		Type	Armour	Quality	Training	Shooting	Close Combat				
Cavalry		Cavalry	Armoured	Superior	Undrilled	–	Light Spear, Swordsmen	16	4	0–4	
			Armoured	Average				12			
			Protected	Superior				12			
			Protected	Average				9			
Hoplites	Any date	Heavy Foot	Armoured	Average	Undrilled	–	Offensive Spearmen	9	6–8	6–8	
	Only from 405	Heavy Foot	Armoured	Average	Drilled	–	Offensive Spearmen	10	6–8		
Other foot	Any date	Medium Foot	Protected	Average	Undrilled	–	Light Spear, Swordsmen	6	6–8	6–24	
	Only from 405	Medium Foot	Protected	Average	Drilled	–	Light Spear, Swordsmen	7	6–8		
Skirmishers		Light Foot	Unprotected	Average	Undrilled	Javelins	Light Spear	4	4–6	0–6	

ITALIAN HILL TRIBES

This list covers the various Italian hill tribes, including the Aequi, Aurunci, Hernici, Picentes, Sabines, Sidicini and Volsci from the early 7th century BC until the last of these were conquered by Rome in the early 3rd century BC.

Volsci Picked Infantryman

It also covers the Samnites prior to the formation of the Samnite League in 355 BC. It is part of the "Seven Hills" theme, and can also be used in themed tournaments based on Field of Glory Companion 1: *Rise of Rome*.

TROOP NOTES

Infantry and cavalry fought mainly with javelins and swords.

ITALIAN HILL TRIBE STARTER ARMY

Commander-in-Chief	1	Field Commander
Sub-commanders	2	2 x Troop Commander
Cavalry	2 BGs	Each comprising 4 bases of cavalry: Superior, Protected, Undrilled Cavalry – Light Spear, Swordsmen
Picked javelinmen	2 BGs	Each comprising 6 bases of picked javelinmen: Superior, Protected, Undrilled Medium Foot – Impact Foot, Swordsmen
Javelinmen	4 BGs	Each comprising 8 bases of javelinmen: Average, Protected, Undrilled Medium Foot – Impact Foot, Swordsmen
Skirmishers	2 BGs	Each comprising 6 bases of skirmishers: Average, Unprotected, Undrilled Light Foot – Javelins, Light Spear
Camp	1	Unfortified camp
Total	10 BGs	Camp, 8 mounted bases, 56 foot bases, 3 commanders

BUILDING A CUSTOMISED LIST USING OUR ARMY POINTS

Choose an army based on the maxima and minima in the list below. The following special instructions apply to this army:

- Commanders should be depicted as cavalry or javelinmen.

- A hill tribe allied commander's contingent must conform to the Italian Hill Tribes allies list below, but the troops in the contingent are deducted from the minima and maxima in the main list.
- All Medium Foot javelinmen must have the same close combat capabilities.

ITALIAN HILL TRIBES									
Territory Types: Agricultural, Hilly, Woodland									
C-in-C	Inspired Commander/Field Commander/Troop Commander						80/50/35	1	
Sub-commanders	Field Commander						50	0–2	
	Troop Commander						35	0–3	
Hill tribe allied commanders	Field Commander/Troop Commander						40/25	0–2	
Troop name	Troop Type				Capabilities		Points per base	Bases per BG	Total bases
	Type	Armour	Quality	Training	Shooting	Close Combat			
Core Troops									
Cavalry	Cavalry	Protected	Superior	Undrilled	–	Light Spear, Swordsmen	12	4–6	4–8
			Average				9		
Picked javelinmen	Medium Foot	Protected	Superior	Undrilled	–	Light Spear, Swordsmen	8	6–8	0–16
	Medium Foot	Protected	Superior	Undrilled	–	Impact Foot, Swordsmen	9	6–8	
Javelinmen	Medium Foot	Protected	Average	Undrilled	–	Light Spear, Swordsmen	6	6–8	16–160
	Medium Foot	Protected	Average	Undrilled	–	Impact Foot, Swordsmen	7	6–8	
Optional Troops									
Skirmishers	Light Foot	Unprotected	Average	Undrilled	Javelins	Light Spear	4	6–8	0–16
Field fortifications	Field Fortifications						3		0–16
Allies									
Latin allies (Only before 338)									

Note: Total bases for Core Troops overall is 24–160.

ITALIAN HILL TRIBE ALLIES									
Allied commander	Field Commander/Troop Commander						40/25	1	
Troop name	Troop Type				Capabilities		Points per base	Bases per BG	Total bases
	Type	Armour	Quality	Training	Shooting	Close Combat			
Cavalry	Cavalry	Protected	Superior	Undrilled	–	Light Spear, Swordsmen	12	4	0–4
			Average				9		
Picked javelinmen	Medium Foot	Protected	Superior	Undrilled	–	Light Spear, Swordsmen	8	4–6	0–6
	Medium Foot	Protected	Superior	Undrilled	–	Impact Foot, Swordsmen	9	4–6	
Javelinmen	Medium Foot	Protected	Average	Undrilled	–	Light Spear, Swordsmen	6	6–8	6–32
	Medium Foot	Protected	Average	Undrilled	–	Impact Foot, Swordsmen	7	6–8	
Skirmishers	Light Foot	Unprotected	Average	Undrilled	Javelins	Light Spear	4	4–6	0–6

Note: Total bases for Allies overall is 8–32.

Venetic warriors, by Richard Hook. Taken from Men-At-Arms 283: Early Roman Armies.

LATIN

This list covers Latin armies from 509 BC until the end of the Latin War in 338 BC. It is part of the "Seven Hills" theme, and can also be used in themed tournaments based on Field of Glory Companion 1: *Rise of Rome*.

The Latin League, probably formed in the 7th century BC, was a mutual defence confederation of Latin-speaking people in the region of Latium (modern Lazio) near Rome. Following the legendary Battle of Lake Regillus, in which the Latin League, led by the exiled King of Rome,

Tarquinius Superbus, was defeated by the army of the Roman Republic, a treaty of alliance was signed in 493 BC between Rome and the League.

This treaty provided for mutual defence against the neighbouring hill tribes. Joint forces were to be commanded by Roman generals.

Over the next 150 years, as the power of Rome grew, it increasingly came to dominate the League. This eventually led to Latin rebellion in the Latin War

Latin Officers

(340–338 BC). Following Roman victory, the League was dissolved and the Latin towns were directly ruled from Rome. The Latins were granted varying degrees of Roman citizenship.

TROOP NOTES

Livy describes the Latins as identical to the Romans in language, customs, arms and military institutions.

LATIN STARTER ARMY (405–338 BC)		
Commander-in-Chief	1	Field Commander
Sub-commanders	2	2 x Troop Commander
Cavalry	3 BGs	Each comprising 4 bases of cavalry: Average, Armoured, Undrilled Cavalry – Light Spear, Swordsmen
Separately deployed infantry of the 1st class	2 BGs	Each comprising 6 bases of infantry of the 1st class: Average, Armoured, Drilled Heavy Foot – Offensive Spearmen
Separately deployed infantry of the 2nd or 3rd class	3 BGs	Each comprising 6 bases of infantry of the 2nd or 3rd class: Average, Protected, Drilled Heavy Foot – Offensive Spearmen
Infantry of the 4th class	2 BGs	Each comprising 6 bases of infantry of the 4th class: Average, Unprotected, Undrilled Light Foot – Javelins, Light Spear
Infantry of the 5th class	1 BG	6 bases of infantry of the 5th class: Average, Unprotected, Undrilled Light Foot – Sling
Camp	1	Unfortified camp
Total	11 BGs	Camp, 12 mounted bases, 48 foot bases, 3 commanders

BUILDING A CUSTOMISED LIST USING OUR ARMY POINTS

Choose an army based on the maxima and minima in the list below. The following special instructions apply:

- Commanders should be depicted as cavalry.
- Cavalry can always dismount as Superior, Armoured or Protected (as mounted type), Undrilled, Heavy Foot, Impact Foot, Swordsmen.
- 1st class infantry must either all be deployed separately or all be deployed in mixed battle groups with 2nd and 3rd class infantry.
- If deployed separately, the army cannot include more battle groups of 1st class infantry than it includes of 2nd and 3rd class infantry.
- The minima marked * only apply if the Heavy Foot classes are deployed separately.
- The minimum marked ** only applies if mixed bodies of 1st, 2nd and 3rd class infantry are used.
- If any 1st, 2nd or 3rd class infantry are Drilled, all must be.
- Only one allied contingent can be used.

5th class Infantryman

Early Roman warriors, by Richard Hook. Taken from *Men-At-Arms 283: Early Roman Armies*.

LATIN

Territory Types: Agricultural, Developed

C-in-C		Inspired Commander/Field Commander/Troop Commander						80/50/35		1	
Sub-commanders		Field Commander						50		0–2	
		Troop Commander						35		0–3	
Troop name		**Troop Type**				**Capabilities**		**Points per base**		**Bases per BG**	**Total bases**
		Type	Armour	Quality	Training	Shooting	Close Combat				
Core Troops											
Cavalry		Cavalry	Armoured	Average	Undrilled	–	Light Spear, Swordsmen	12		4–6	4–12
			Protected					9			
Separately deployed infantry of the 1st class	Any date	Heavy Foot	Armoured	Average	Undrilled	–	Offensive Spearmen	9		6–8	*8–24
	Only from 405	Heavy Foot	Armoured	Average	Drilled	–	Offensive Spearmen	10		6–8	
Separately deployed infantry of the 2nd or 3rd class	Any date	Heavy Foot	Protected	Average	Undrilled	–	Offensive Spearmen	7		6–8	*8–88
	Only from 405	Heavy Foot	Protected	Average	Drilled	–	Offensive Spearmen	8		6–8	
Mixed infantry of the 1st, 2nd and 3rd classes	Any date	Heavy Foot	Armoured	Average	Undrilled	–	Offensive Spearmen	9		6–8	0–32 / **20–118
	Only from 405	Heavy Foot	Armoured	Average	Drilled	–	Offensive Spearmen	10		6–8	
	Any date	Heavy Foot	Protected	Average	Undrilled	–	Offensive Spearmen	7		6–8	0–118
	Only from 405	Heavy Foot	Protected	Average	Drilled	–	Offensive Spearmen	8		6–8	
Infantry of the 4th class		Medium Foot	Protected	Average	Undrilled	–	Light Spear	5		6–8	6–24
			Unprotected					4			
		Light Foot	Unprotected	Average	Undrilled	Javelins	Light Spear	4		6–8	
Infantry of the 5th class		Light Foot	Unprotected	Average	Undrilled	Sling	–	4		6–8	6–16
				Poor				2			
		Light Foot	Unprotected	Average	Undrilled	Javelins	Light Spear	4		6–8	
				Poor				2			
Allies											
Campanian allies											
Italian Hill Tribe allies											

LATIN ALLIES

Allied commander		Field Commander/Troop Commander					40/25		1	
Troop name		Troop Type				Capabilities		Points per base	Bases per BG	Total bases
		Type	Armour	Quality	Training	Shooting	Close Combat			
Cavalry		Cavalry	Armoured	Average	Undrilled	–	Light Spear, Swordsmen	12	4–6	4–6
			Protected					9		
Separately deployed infantry of the 1st class	Any date	Heavy Foot	Armoured	Average	Undrilled	–	Offensive Spearmen	9	6–8	*6–8
	Only from 405	Heavy Foot	Armoured	Average	Drilled	–	Offensive Spearmen	10	6–8	
Separately deployed infantry of the 2nd or 3rd class	Any date	Heavy Foot	Protected	Average	Undrilled	–	Offensive Spearmen	7	6–8	*6–16
	Only from 405	Heavy Foot	Protected	Average	Drilled	–	Offensive Spearmen	8	6–8	
Mixed infantry of the 1st, 2nd and 3rd classes	Any date	Heavy Foot	Armoured	Average	Undrilled	–	Offensive Spearmen	9	6–8	0–12	**8–24
	Only from 405	Heavy Foot	Armoured	Average	Drilled	–	Offensive Spearmen	10	6–8	
	Any date	Heavy Foot	Protected	Average	Undrilled	–	Offensive Spearmen	7	6–8	0–24
	Only from 405	Heavy Foot	Protected	Average	Drilled	–	Offensive Spearmen	8	6–8	
Infantry of the 4th class		Medium Foot	Protected	Average	Undrilled	–	Light Spear	5	6–8	6–8	6–12
			Unprotected					4		
		Light Foot	Unprotected	Average	Undrilled	Javelins	Light Spear	4	6–8	
Infantry of the 5th class		Light Foot	Unprotected	Average	Undrilled	Sling	–	4	4–6	0–6
				Poor				2		
		Light Foot	Unprotected	Average	Undrilled	Javelins	Light Spear	4	4–6	
				Poor				2		

SAMNITE

This list covers Samnite armies from 355 to 272 BC. It is part of the "Seven Hills" theme, and can also be used in themed tournaments based on Field of Glory Companion 1: Rise of Rome.

The Samnites were one of the Oscan peoples who lived in central and southern Italy. They occupied the south central Apennines, bordering on Latium to the north, Lucania to the south, Campania to the west and Apulia to the east.

A written treaty with the Romans was made in 354 BC. Soon after, in 343 BC, the First Samnite war against Rome broke out, in response to Samnite incursions into Campania. Roman and Latin forces fought alongside Campanians against the Samnites. The Samnites were defeated by 341 BC. Soon after, war broke out between

the Romans and their Latin "allies". The Romans then allied with the Samnites against the Latins and Campanians. Once again, the Roman side was victorious.

In 327 BC, the Samnites again entered Campania, and put a garrison into Neapolis (modern Naples). The Campanians again sought Roman aid, and so the Second Samnite War (326–304 BC) began. In 321 BC, having come off worst in the fighting, the Samnites sued for peace – but were offered such harsh terms that they felt obliged to refuse. The Romans were given cause to regret their rapacity. Later the same year, at the Caudine Forks, the Samnites trapped the Roman army in a mountain valley, where it began to starve. The consuls were forced to agree to the terms offered by the Samnite leader, Gaius Pontius, whereby a five-year peace treaty was agreed on terms favourable to the Samnites, 600 Roman equites were handed over as hostages and the whole Roman army was forced to undergo the humiliating ritual of "passing under the yoke". Although this halted the war for five years, it left the Romans unweakened and thirsting for revenge.

When the war began again, the Samnites were initially successful, defeating the Romans at Lautulae in 315 BC. In 311 BC the Etruscans came into the war on the side of the Samnites. Thereafter the tide of the war turned in the Romans' favour, and they inflicted a series of defeats on their opponents. The Etruscans sued for peace in 308 and the Samnites in 304 BC.

The Third Samnite War began in 298 BC with the Samnites allied to the Etruscans, Umbrians and Gauls in a last ditch attempt by all of Rome's neighbours to halt the expansion of her power. The decisive battle was fought at Sentinum in 295 BC between the Romans and the combined Samnite and Gallic forces, the latter including chariots. The Etruscan and Umbrian armies were not present, having been drawn off to face subsidiary Roman forces. After initial setbacks the Romans were victorious, inflicting heavy losses

Samnite warriors, by Richard Hook. Taken from Men-At-Arms 283: Early Roman Armies.

on their opponents in the pursuit. The Etruscans soon sued for peace, but the Samnites fought on doggedly until 290 BC when the Romans granted them surprisingly lenient peace terms.

In the Pyrrhic war, the Samnites joined Pyrrhos' coalition, remaining in arms until 272 BC, long after Pyrrhos had returned to Epiros.

TROOP NOTES

Samnite foot were more lightly equipped than their Roman enemies, and were fond of fighting in hills and woodland, preferably from ambush. Helmets were the norm. The commonest shield was the oval *scutum* – similar to the Roman type, but somewhat smaller. A proportion of men wore small metal breastplates, but most lacked body armour. They fought with javelins and sword. Livy (echoed by Frontinus) describes them as particularly strong in the initial attack, but lacking staying power. We therefore classify them as Medium Foot, Protected, Impact Foot, Swordsmen.

The army was organised into legions, possibly larger than Roman ones. Each legion was divided into cohorts, possibly 400 strong. There is no evidence that they used multi-line formations like the Romans.

The elite "Linen Legion" which fought at Aquilonia in 293 BC was 16,000 strong. It was raised from picked men and its members swore an oath never to flee. Similar bodies may have been raised in earlier campaigns.

About half of the cavalry in Oscan tomb paintings wear metal armour. Others wear linen or leather armour. Most lack shields, at least in the earlier part of the period. We give the option of classifying Samnite cavalry as Armoured or Protected. They fought with javelins and swords.

The Samnites were too poor to hire mercenaries, but often fought in alliance with other Italian peoples.

Samnite Skirmisher

SAMNITE STARTER ARMY		
Commander-in-Chief	1	Troop Commander
Sub-commanders	2	2 x Troop Commander
Cavalry	2 BGs	Each comprising 4 bases of cavalry: Superior, Armoured, Undrilled Cavalry – Light Spear, Swordsmen
Linen Legion	3 BGs	Each comprising 6 bases of Linen Legion: Superior, Protected, Drilled Medium Foot – Impact Foot, Swordsmen
Other foot	3 BGs	Each comprising 6 bases of other foot: Average, Protected, Drilled Medium Foot – Impact Foot, Swordsmen
Skirmishers	1 BG	8 bases of skirmishers: Average, Protected, Drilled Light Foot – Javelins, Light Spear
Camp	1	Unfortified camp
Total	9 BGs	Camp, 8 mounted bases, 44 foot bases, 3 commanders

BUILDING A CUSTOMISED LIST USING OUR ARMY POINTS

Choose an army based on the maxima and minima in the list below. The following special instructions apply to this army:

- Commanders should be depicted as cavalry, Linen Legion or other foot.
- Gallic, Etruscan and Umbrian allies can be used together from 330, otherwise only one allied contingent can be used. No allies are permitted after 281.

SAMNITE									
Territory Types: Agricultural, Hilly, Woodland									
C-in-C	Inspired Commander/Field Commander/Troop Commander						80/50/35	1	
Sub-commanders	Field Commander						50	0–2	
	Troop Commander						35	0–3	
Troop name	Troop Type				Capabilities		Points per base	Bases per BG	Total bases
	Type	Armour	Quality	Training	Shooting	Close Combat			
Core Troops									
Cavalry	Cavalry	Armoured	Superior	Undrilled	–	Light Spear, Swordsmen	16	4–6	4–12
	Armoured	Average					12		
	Protected	Superior					12		
	Protected	Average					9		
Linen Legion or equivalent	Medium Foot	Protected	Superior	Drilled	–	Impact Foot, Swordsmen	10	6–8	0–32	24–112
Other foot	Medium Foot	Protected	Average	Drilled	–	Impact Foot, Swordsmen	8	6–8	16–112
Optional Troops									
Skirmishers	Light Foot	Protected	Average	Drilled	Javelins	Light Spear	5	6–8	0–16
		Unprotected					4		
Field fortifications	Field Fortifications						3		0–16
Fortified camp	Only from 280						24		0–1
Allies									
Apulian allies – Apulian, Lucanian or Bruttian									
Campanian allies									
Etruscan allies									
Gallic allies – See Field of Glory Companion 1: Rise of Rome									
Roman allies (Only in 340) – Early Republican Roman									
Umbrian allies									
Volsci and/or Hernici allies – Italian Hill Tribes									

Allied commander	Troop Type				Capabilities		Points per base	Bases per BG	Total bases
SAMNITE ALLIES									
Allied commander	Field Commander/Troop Commander						40/25	1	
Troop name	Type	Armour	Quality	Training	Shooting	Close Combat			
Cavalry	Cavalry	Armoured	Superior	Undrilled	–	Light Spear, Swordsmen	16	4	0–4
	Armoured	Average					12		
	Protected	Superior					12		
	Protected	Average					9		
Linen Legion or equivalent	Medium Foot	Protected	Superior	Drilled	–	Impact Foot, Swordsmen	10	6–8	0–12 } 8–32
Other foot	Medium Foot	Protected	Average	Drilled	–	Impact Foot, Swordsmen	8	6–8	6–32
Skirmishers	Light Foot	Protected	Average	Drilled	Javelins	Light Spear	5	4–6	0–6
		Unprotected					4		

CAMPANIAN

This list covers Campanian armies from the late 5th century BC until 211 BC. It is part of the "Seven Hills" theme, and can also be used in themed tournaments based on Field of Glory Companion 1: *Rise of Rome*.

The Campani, an Oscan people, gained control of the Greek and Etruscan cities of the northern part of the Campanian plain towards the end of the 5th century BC, forming the Campanian League. In the south, Neapolis (Naples) remained Greek, and Oscan Nola remained independent, allied with the Samnites.

In 343 BC, threatened by Samnite incursions, the Campanians invited Roman intervention, resulting in the First Samnite War. When a peace was agreed between the Romans and Samnites, that threatened to carve up Italy between them, the Campanians joined the Latins in revolt. At the end of the Latin War in 338 BC, the Campanians were made Roman citizens, although only the nobles (who had stayed out of the war) gained voting rights.

In 327 BC, the Samnites established a garrison in Neapolis. The Campanians once again sought Roman aid, resulting in the Second Samnite War (326–304 BC). During this war, Nola remained allied with the Samnites. Thereafter, Campania remained loyal to Rome until the Second Punic War.

Following the Roman defeat by the Carthaginians at the Battle of Cannae in 216 BC, Capua joined Hannibal against Rome, along with most of southern Italy. In contrast, Nola offered Hannibal defiance. Capua fell to the Romans in 211 BC, after a prolonged siege.

TROOP NOTES

Campanian armies included the usual Oscan javelinmen and also, influenced by the culture of the formerly Greek and Etruscan cities of the Campanian plain, hoplites. We assume that Nolan forces would be similar.

Campanian Hoplite

From 338 BC, the Campanians were Roman citizens, and came to adopt Roman tactics – though possibly not immediately.

The Campanian plain was excellent for horse breeding, and Campanian cavalry were famously effective. About half of the cavalry in Oscan tomb paintings wear metal armour. Others wear linen or leather armour. Most lack shields, at least in the earlier part of the period. We give the option of classifying Campanian cavalry as Armoured or Protected. They fought with javelins and swords.

Campanian Cavalry

CAMPANIAN STARTER ARMY (BEFORE 275 BC)		
Commander-in-Chief	1	Field Commander
Sub-commanders	2	2 x Troop Commander
Cavalry	2 BGs	Each comprising 4 bases of cavalry: Superior, Armoured, Undrilled Cavalry – Light Spear, Swordsmen
Cavalry	1 BG	4 bases of cavalry: Superior, Protected, Undrilled Cavalry – Light Spear, Swordsmen
Hoplites	2 BGs	Each comprising 8 bases of hoplites: Average, Protected, Drilled Heavy Foot – Offensive Spearmen
Javelinmen	3 BGs	Each comprising 6 bases of Javelinmen: Average, Protected, Drilled Medium Foot – Light Spear, Swordsmen
Skirmishers	2 BGs	Each comprising 6 bases of skirmishers: Average, Unprotected, Drilled Light Foot – Javelins, Light Spear
Camp	1	Unfortified camp
Total	10 BGs	Camp, 12 mounted bases, 46 foot bases, 3 commanders

BUILDING A CUSTOMISED LIST USING OUR ARMY POINTS

Choose an army based on the maxima and minima in the list below. The following special instructions apply to this army:

- Commanders should be depicted as cavalry.
- The minima marked * only apply before 337.
- The minimum marked ** only applies from 275.

- Hoplites cannot be used with *hastati*, *principes* or *triarii*.
- *Hastati & Principes*: Triarii: Skirmishers quality must either be Average: Superior: Average, Average: Average: Average, Poor: Average: Poor or Poor: Poor: Poor.
- Samnite allies cannot be used with Roman or Latin allies. No allies are permitted after 281.

CAMPANIAN

Territory Types: Agricultural

C-in-C	Inspired Commander/Field Commander/Troop Commander					80/50/35	1	
Sub-commanders	Field Commander					50	0–2	
	Troop Commander					35	0–3	

Troop name		Troop Type				Capabilities		Points per base	Bases per BG	Total bases
		Type	Armour	Quality	Training	Shooting	Close Combat			
Core Troops										
Cavalry		Cavalry	Armoured	Superior	Undrilled	–	Light Spear, Swordsmen	16	4–6	4–16
			Protected					12		
Javelinmen	Only before 275	Medium Foot	Protected	Average	Undrilled	–	Light Spear, Swordsmen	6	6–8	*12–64
				Average	Drilled			7		
				Poor	Undrilled			4		
				Poor	Drilled			5		
Hoplites		Heavy Foot	Protected	Average	Undrilled	–	Offensive Spearmen	7	6–8	*12–48
				Average	Drilled			8		
				Poor	Undrilled			5		
				Poor	Drilled			6		
Hastati & Principes	Only from 337	Heavy Foot	Protected	Average	Drilled	–	Impact Foot, Swordsmen	8	4–8	**16–80
				Poor				6		
Triarii		Heavy Foot	Protected	Superior	Drilled	–	Offensive Spearmen	10	2–4	1 per 4 hastati and principes
				Average				8		
				Poor				6		
Optional Troops										
Skirmishers		Light Foot	Unprotected	Average	Undrilled	Javelins	Light Spear	4	6–8	0–24
				Poor				2		
Fortified camp	Only from 280							24		0–1
Allies										
Latin allies (Only from 343 to 338)										
Roman allies (Only from 343) – Early Republican Roman										
Samnite allies										

CAMPANIAN ALLIES

Allied commander	Field Commander/Troop Commander					40/25	1	

Troop name		Troop Type				Capabilities		Points per base	Bases per BG	Total bases
		Type	Armour	Quality	Training	Shooting	Close Combat			
Cavalry		Cavalry	Armoured	Superior	Undrilled	–	Light Spear, Swordsmen	16	4–6	4–6
			Protected					12		
Javelinmen	Only before 275	Medium Foot	Protected	Average	Undrilled	–	Light Spear, Swordsmen	6	6–8	*6–20
				Average	Drilled			7		
				Poor	Undrilled			4		
				Poor	Drilled			5		
Hoplites		Heavy Foot	Protected	Average	Undrilled	–	Offensive Spearmen	7	6–8	*6–16
				Average	Drilled			8		
				Poor	Undrilled			5		
				Poor	Drilled			6		
Hastati & Principes	Only from 337	Heavy Foot	Protected	Average	Drilled	–	Impact Foot, Swordsmen	8	4–8	**8–24
				Poor				6		
Triarii		Heavy Foot	Protected	Superior	Drilled	–	Offensive Spearmen	10	2–4	1 per 4 hastati and principes
				Average				8		
				Poor				6		
Skirmishers		Light Foot	Unprotected	Average	Undrilled	Javelins	Light Spear	4	6–8	0–8
				Poor				2		

Samnite and wounded Lucanian heavy infantrymen, and Campanian cavalryman, by Richard Hook. Taken from *Men-At-Arms* 121: Armies of the Carthaginian Wars 265–146 BC.

APULIAN, LUCANIAN OR BRUTTIAN

This list covers Apulian and Lucanian armies from the 5th century, and Bruttian armies from the 4th century BC, until 203 BC. It is part of the "Seven Hills" theme, and can also be used in themed tournaments based on Field of Glory Companion 1: *Rise of Rome*.

Apulia, in south-east Italy, was occupied by three tribes of mixed Illyrian and Oscan origin. In the heel of Italy were the Messapii, while further north were the Peucetii and Dauni. Generally the Messapii aligned with the Samnites, while the Dauni and Peucetii, under threat of Samnite expansion, aligned with Rome. The Messapii allied with Pyrrhos in the Pyrrhic War.

The Lucani, an Oscan people, conquered Lucania (the region just north of the toe of Italy) in the mid-5th century BC. They also conquered the toe of Italy, and reduced the former inhabitants – the Oenotrians – to vassalage. In 298 BC they allied with Rome against the Samnites. They allied with Pyrrhos in the Pyrrhic War and some allied with Hannibal in the Second Punic War.

The Bruttii, in the toe of Italy (modern Calabria) arose as a result of a revolt by the Oenotrians against the Lucanians in the mid-4th century BC. Their independence was soon recognised, and within 30 years the two peoples were allied against their Greek neighbours. In 326 BC a combined Lucanian and Bruttian army defeated and killed King Alexander of Epirus at Pandosia. Around 300 BC Bruttium came under attack by Agathokles of Syracuse. After initial successes the Syracusan forces were repelled.

Subsequently the Bruttians allied with Pyrrhos and then Hannibal against Rome.

TROOP NOTES

Apulian, Lucanian and Bruttian armies largely consisted of the usual Oscan javelinmen. However, the Apulians tended to carry a large, round hoplite-style shield instead of the oval *scutum*, and the Lucanians and Bruttians may also have used round shields. More Lucanian foot may have had metal body armour than amongst the other Oscans. Battle groups rated as Armoured are those with a high proportion of such armoured men.

The Apulians had the highest proportion of cavalry of any of the Oscan peoples. Many are depicted unarmoured and shieldless. Others have shields and/or armour.

Apulian Javelinmen

LUCANIAN STARTER ARMY

Commander-in-Chief	1	Troop Commander
Sub-commanders	2	2 x Troop Commander
Cavalry	2 BGs	Each comprising 4 bases of cavalry: Superior, Armoured, Undrilled Cavalry – Light Spear, Swordsmen
Armoured javelinmen	3 BGs	Each comprising 6 bases of armoured javelinmen: Average, Armoured, Drilled Medium Foot – Light Spear, Swordsmen
Other javelinmen	4 BGs	Each comprising 6 bases of other javelinmen: Average, Protected, Drilled Medium Foot – Light Spear, Swordsmen
Skirmishers	2 BGs	Each comprising 8 bases of skirmishers: Poor, Unprotected, Drilled Light Foot – Javelins, Light Spear
Camp	1	Unfortified camp
Total	11 BGs	Camp, 8 mounted bases, 58 foot bases, 3 commanders

BUILDING A CUSTOMISED LIST USING OUR ARMY POINTS

Choose an army based on the maxima and minima in the list below. The following special instructions apply to this army:

- Commanders should be depicted as cavalry.

APULIAN, LUCANIAN OR BRUTTIAN

Territory Types: Apulians – Agricultural, Hilly. Lucanians – Agricultural, Hilly, Woodland. Bruttians – Hilly, Woodland.

C-in-C								
	Inspired Commander/Field Commander/Troop Commander					80/50/35		1
Sub-commanders	Field Commander					50		0–2
	Troop Commander					35		0–3

Troop name		Troop Type				Capabilities		Points per base	Bases per BG	Total bases
		Type	Armour	Quality	Training	Shooting	Close Combat			
Core Troops										
Cavalry	Only Apulians	Cavalry	Armoured	Superior	Undrilled	–	Light Spear, Swordsmen	16	4–6	4–12
			Protected					12		
		Cavalry	Unprotected	Superior	Undrilled	–	Light Spear, Swordsmen	10	4–6	4–16	8–24
				Average				8		
	Only Lucanians or Bruttians	Cavalry	Armoured	Superior	Undrilled	–	Light Spear, Swordsmen	16	4–6	4–12
			Armoured	Average				12		
			Protected	Superior				12		
			Protected	Average				9		
Javelinmen	Any	Medium Foot	Protected	Average	Undrilled	–	Light Spear, Swordsmen	6	6–8	12–128	18–128
					Drilled			7		
	Only Lucanians	Medium Foot	Armoured	Average	Undrilled	–	Light Spear, Swordsmen	8	6–8	0–24
					Drilled			9		
Optional Troops										
Skirmishers		Light Foot	Unprotected	Average	Undrilled	Javelins	Light Spear	4	6–8	0–24
				Poor				2		
Fortified camp	Only from 280							24		0–1
Allies										
Only Bruttians										
Lucanian allies – Apulian, Lucanian or Bruttian										
Only Lucanians										
Bruttian allies – Apulian, Lucanian or Bruttian										
Roman allies (Only from 298 to 290) – Early Republican Roman										

APULIAN, LUCANIAN OR BRUTTIAN ALLIES

Allied commander		Field Commander/Troop Commander					40/25		1	
Troop name		Troop Type				Capabilities		Points per base	Bases per BG	Total bases
		Type	Armour	Quality	Training	Shooting	Close Combat			
Cavalry	Only Apulians	Cavalry	Armoured	Superior	Undrilled	–	Light Spear, Swordsmen	16	4	4
			Protected					12		
		Cavalry	Unprotected	Superior	Undrilled	–	Light Spear, Swordsmen	10	4	0–4
				Average				8		
	Only Lucanians or Bruttians	Cavalry	Armoured	Superior	Undrilled	–	Light Spear, Swordsmen	16	4	0–4
			Armoured	Average				12		
			Protected	Superior				12		
			Protected	Average				9		
Javelinmen	Any	Medium Foot	Protected	Average	Undrilled	–	Light Spear, Swordsmen	6	6–8	6–24
					Drilled			7		6–24
	Only Lucanians	Medium Foot	Armoured	Average	Undrilled	–	Light Spear, Swordsmen	8	6–8	0–8
					Drilled			9		
Skirmishers		Light Foot	Unprotected	Average	Undrilled	Javelins	Light Spear	4	6–8	0–8
				Poor				2		

EARLY NOMAD

This list covers the various nomad and semi-nomadic tribes of the desert and steppe areas bordering Syria, Canaan and Mesopotamia from 3100 BC until the widespread adoption of the horse towards the end of the 4th century BC. It can be used in themed tournaments based on Field of Glory Companion 9: *Swifter than Eagles*.

Amongst the most successful of these early nomads were the Amorites, who moved into Mesopotamia and Syria in the second half of the 3rd millennium BC, precipitating a collapse of the city state structure, especially in Syria and Canaan. At the start of the 2nd millennium BC the Amorites founded a number of kingdoms, including Assyria, and these are covered by the Amorite Kingdoms list.

This list also includes the Hebrews from their leaving Egypt, the period of wandering in the desert and arrival in Canaan until King David ascended the throne *c*.1000 BC. After their settlement in Canaan the Hebrews often found themselves at a disadvantage in open warfare against enemies who used chariots and were thus often forced to use hilly country as a counter.

The Early Nomad allies list in this book can be used instead of the Early Nomad and Proto-Arab allies lists in *Swifter than Eagles*.

TROOP NOTES

Large army-sized groups of nomads would have been formed from alliances of a number of tribes, although individual tribes could on occasion field large numbers.

From about the start of the first millennium BC, early proto-Arab tribes such as the Midianites and Amalekites

Midianite Camel-mounted Warriors

started to use camels in warfare. Some Assyrian depictions show two riders, but this does not affect their classification or capabilities. Other Assyrian depictions show infantry fighting from behind tethered camels in a similar manner to the later Moors and so these tethered camels are treated in the same way as they are in that list.

EARLY NOMAD STARTER ARMY (AFTER 1000 BC)		
Commander-in-Chief	1	Field Commander
Sub-commanders	2	2 x Troop Commander
Camel-mounted warriors	6 BGs	Each comprising 4 bases of camel-mounted warriors: Average, Unprotected, Undrilled Camelry – Bow
Warriors	3 BGs	Each comprising 8 bases of warriors: Average, Protected, Undrilled Medium Foot – Light Spear, Swordsmen
Skirmishers	1 BG	6 bases of skirmishers: Average, Unprotected, Undrilled Light Foot – Javelins, Light Spear
Skirmishers	1 BG	8 bases of skirmishers: Average, Unprotected, Undrilled Light Foot – Bow
Skirmishers	1 BG	8 bases of skirmishers: Average, Unprotected, Undrilled Light Foot – Sling
Camp	1	Unfortified camp
Total	12 BGs	Camp, 24 mounted bases, 46 foot bases, 3 commanders

BUILDING A CUSTOMISED LIST USING OUR ARMY POINTS

Choose an army based on the maxima and minima in the list below. The following special instructions apply to this army:

- Commanders should be depicted as warriors or, after 1800, in a 2-horse chariot, or, after 1000, as a camel-mounted warrior.
- An Early Nomad allied commander's contingent must conform to the Early Nomad Allies list below, but the troops in the contingent are deducted from the minima and maxima in the main list.
- Only one city allied contingent can be used.
- Syrian subject city allies from the Amorite Kingdoms list cannot use chariots.
- Tethered camels are treated as Field Fortifications but disorder cavalry as if camelry, and cost extra points as per camelry.
- Hebrews cannot use camels.

EARLY NOMAD

Territory Types: Any but Hebrews in Canaan – Steppe, Desert. Hebrews in Canaan – Agricultural, Hilly			
C-in-C	Inspired Commander/Field Commander/Troop Commander	80/50/35	1
Sub-commanders	Field Commander/Troop Commander	50/35	0–2
Early Nomad allied commanders	Field Commander/Troop Commander	40/25	0–3

Troop name		Troop Type				Capabilities		Points per base	Bases per BG	Total bases
		Type	Armour	Quality	Training	Shooting	Close Combat			
Core Troops										
Warriors	Only before 2500	Medium Foot	Unprotected	Average	Undrilled	–	Light Spear	4	6–10	48–220
	Only from 2500	Medium Foot	Protected	Average	Undrilled	–	Light Spear	5	6–8	24–150
			Unprotected					4		
		Medium Foot	Protected	Average	Undrilled	–	Light Spear, Swordsmen	6	6–8	
Skirmishers		Light Foot	Unprotected	Average	Undrilled	Javelins	Light Spear	4	6–8	6–24 / 8–32
		Light Foot	Unprotected	Average	Undrilled	Sling	–	4	6–8	0–12
		Light Foot	Unprotected	Average	Undrilled	Bow	–	5	6–8	0–12
Camel-mounted warriors	Only from 1000	Camelry	Unprotected	Average	Undrilled	Bow	–	10	4–6	6–36
Optional Troops										
Poor quality warriors	Any date	Medium Foot	Unprotected	Poor	Undrilled	–	Light Spear	2	8–12	0–36
	Only from 2500	Medium Foot	Protected	Poor	Undrilled	–	Light Spear	3	8–12	
Archers		Medium Foot	Unprotected	Average	Undrilled	Bow	–	5	6–8	0–12
Tethered camels	Only from 1000	Field Fortifications						5		0–12
Allies										
Subject Syrian city allies (Only from 2200 to 2001) – Later Sumerian or Akkadian – see Field of Glory Companion 9: *Swifter than Eagles*										
Subject Syrian city allies (Only from 2000 to 1600) – Amorite Kingdoms										
Subject Mesopotamian city allies (Only from 2000 to 1800) – Later Sumerian or Akkadian – see Field of Glory Companion 9: *Swifter than Eagles*										

EARLY NOMAD ALLIES

Allied commander		Field Commander/Troop Commander						40/25	1	
Troop name		Troop Type				Capabilities		Points per base	Bases per BG	Total bases
		Type	Armour	Quality	Training	Shooting	Close Combat			
Warriors	Only before 2500	Medium Foot	Unprotected	Average	Undrilled	–	Light Spear	4	6–10	16–48
	Only from 2500	Medium Foot	Protected	Average	Undrilled	–	Light Spear	5	6–8	8–32
			Unprotected					4		
		Medium Foot	Protected	Average	Undrilled	–	Light Spear, Swordsmen	6	6–8	
Skirmishers		Light Foot	Unprotected	Average	Undrilled	Javelins	Light Spear	4	4–6	0–8
		Light Foot	Unprotected	Average	Undrilled	Sling	–	4	4–6	
		Light Foot	Unprotected	Average	Undrilled	Bow	–	5	4–6	
Camel-mounted warriors	Only from 1000	Camelry	Unprotected	Average	Undrilled	Bow	–	10	4–6	4–12

Early Nomad camelry under attack from Assyrian mounted archers, by Angus McBride.
Taken from Men-At-Arms 109: Ancient Armies of the Middle East.

EARLY HIGHLAND RAIDERS

This list covers the various highland peoples of the Zagros, Taurus and Anatolian uplands from c.3000 BC until c.1000 BC. It can be used in themed tournaments based on Field of Glory Companion 9: *Swifter than Eagles*. It includes the early/middle Bronze Age peoples of the Zagros mountains such as the Guti, Lullubi and early Kassites. It also includes the pre-Mitanni Hurrians of north-east Mesopotamia and the Gasgans (Kaska) of northern Anatolia. All appear in the records of their more settled neighbours as fierce and unpredictable raiders of civilised lands, although many of them did have small towns and cities of their own.

TROOP NOTES

Large army-sized groups of these highlanders would have been formed from alliances of a number of tribes, although individual tribes could on occasion field large numbers.

The early Gutian and Lullubi tribesmen are depicted practically naked or wearing animal skins but without shields and so are rated as Unprotected. Later

Highland Warrior

highland tribesmen appear to have adopted shields and so may be Protected although we still allow less well-equipped warriors to be fielded.

Gasgan armies are noted in some Hittite records as sometimes containing levies as well as the normal warriors. As it is likely that most tribes would contain a proportion of lesser warriors, we allow all to field such troops.

From c.2190 to 2115 BC the Gutians over-ran a large portion of Mesopotamia and ruled some

cities as a warrior aristocracy. This gave them access to the city militias. They also formed alliances with unconquered cities.

The Hurrians were the first highland peoples to adopt the chariot in any numbers and went on to found the Mitannian state which created the *maryannu* chariot system that became the dominant military system in the Middle East for the best part of a millennium.

GASGAN STARTER ARMY (AFTER 1700 BC)

Commander-in-Chief	1	Troop Commander
Sub-commanders	2	2 x Troop Commander
Chariots	1 BG	4 bases of chariots: Superior, Undrilled Light Chariots – Bow
Warriors	5 BGs	Each comprising 8 bases of warriors: Average, Protected, Undrilled Medium Foot – Impact Foot, Swordsmen
Poor quality warriors	2 BGs	Each comprising 12 bases of poor quality warriors: Poor, Unprotected, Undrilled Medium Foot – Light Spear
Skirmishers	2 BGs	Each comprising 6 bases of skirmishers: Average, Unprotected, Undrilled Light Foot – Javelins, Light Spear
Skirmishers	2 BGs	Each comprising 6 bases of skirmishers: Average, Unprotected, Undrilled Light Foot – Sling
Camp	1	Unfortified camp
Total	12 BGs	Camp, 4 mounted bases, 88 foot bases, 3 commanders

BUILDING A CUSTOMISED LIST USING OUR ARMY POINTS

Choose an army based on the maxima and minima in the list below. The following special instructions apply to this army:

• Commanders should be depicted as warriors or, if Gutian from 2190 to 2115, in a 4-equid platform car or 2-equid proto-chariot, or, if early Kassite, Gasgan or Hurrian, in a 2-horse chariot.

• An Early Highland Raider allied commander's contingent must conform to the Early Highland Raider allies list below, but the troops in the contingent are deducted from the minima and maxima in the main list.

• Warriors, other than poor quality or those in an allied contingent, must all have the same close combat capabilities.

EARLY HIGHLAND RAIDERS

Territory Types: Hilly, Mountains

C-in-C	Inspired Commander/Field Commander/Troop Commander						80/50/35		1
Sub-commanders	Field Commander						50		0–2
	Troop Commander						35		
Early Highland Raider allied commanders	Field Commander/Troop Commander						40/25		0–3

Troop name		Troop Type				Capabilities		Points per base	Bases per BG	Total bases
		Type	Armour	Quality	Training	Shooting	Close Combat			
Core Troops										
Warriors	Any date	Medium Foot	Unprotected	Average	Undrilled	–	Impact Foot, Swordsmen	6	6–10	30–120
	Only from 2100	Medium Foot	Protected	Average	Undrilled	–	Impact Foot, Swordsmen	7	6–10	
		Medium Foot	Protected	Average	Undrilled	–	Light Spear, Swordsmen	6	6–10	
Poor quality warriors	Any date	Medium Foot	Unprotected	Average	Undrilled	–	Light Spear	4	8–12	0–72
				Poor				2		
	Only from 2100	Medium Foot	Protected	Average	Undrilled	–	Light Spear	5	8–12	
				Poor				3		
Skirmishers		Light Foot	Unprotected	Average	Undrilled	Javelins	Light Spear	4	6–8	6–36 / 8–48
		Light Foot	Unprotected	Average	Undrilled	Sling	–	4	6–8	0–24
		Light Foot	Unprotected	Average	Undrilled	Bow	–	5	6–8	0–18
Optional Troops										
Chariots	Only Gasgans from 1700 BC	Light Chariots	–	Superior	Undrilled	–	Light Spear	15	4	0–4
	Only Hurrians from 1800BC, or early Kassites or Gasgans from 1700 BC	Light Chariots	–	Superior	Undrilled	Bow	–	17	4	
Special Campaigns										
Guti ruling Mesopotamian city states from 2190 to 2115 BC										
Mesopotamian retained spearmen		Heavy Foot	Protected	Average	Drilled	–	Defensive Spearmen	7	6–8	0–12
				Superior				9		
		Medium Foot	Unprotected	Average	Drilled	–	Offensive Spearmen	7	6–8	
				Superior				8		
Mesopotamian militia spearmen		Heavy Foot	Protected	Average	Drilled	–	Defensive Spearmen	7	6–10	12–36
				Poor				5		

Subject city allies – Later Sumerian or Akkadian – see Field of Glory Companion 9: *Swifter than Eagles*

EARLY HIGHLAND RAIDER ALLIES

Allied commander		Field Commander/Troop Commander						40/25		1	
Troop name		Troop Type				Capabilities		Points per base	Bases per BG	Total bases	
		Type	Armour	Quality	Training	Shooting	Close Combat				
Warriors	Any	Medium Foot	Unprotected	Average	Undrilled	–	Impact Foot, Swordsmen	6	6–10	12–36	
	Only from 2100	Medium Foot	Protected	Average	Undrilled	–	Impact Foot, Swordsmen	7	6–10		
		Medium Foot	Protected	Average	Undrilled	–	Light Spear, Swordsmen	6	6–10		
Poor quality warriors	Any	Medium Foot	Unprotected	Average	Undrilled	–	Light Spear	4	8–12	0–24	
				Poor				2			
	Only from 2100	Medium Foot	Protected	Average	Undrilled	–	Light Spear	5	8–12		
				Poor				3			
Skirmishers		Light Foot	Unprotected	Average	Undrilled	Javelins	Light Spear	4	6–8	6–12	6–16
		Light Foot	Unprotected	Average	Undrilled	Sling	–	4	6–8	0–8	
		Light Foot	Unprotected	Average	Undrilled	Bow	–	5	6–8	0–8	

EARLY ELAMITE

This list covers armies from highland Elam, Anshan and Awan as well as the lowland region of Susiana, all located in modern south-west Iran, from c.2800 BC to c.1100 BC (We use the term Elamite to cover all of these, as was often the case with their historical neighbours.). It can be used in themed tournaments based on Field of Glory Companion 9: *Swifter than Eagles*.

During the 3rd millennium BC the various regions were usually independent of each other, although occasionally one would gain ascendancy over the others. However, by the middle of the 2nd millennium BC there was a recognised king of Susa and Anshan (alternatively Anshan and Susa). These and subsequent dynasties were closely associated with the Kassite rulers of Babylon and marriage alliances were common. Ironically, despite these close ties, it was the Babylonian king Nebuchadnezzar I who

Militia Spearman

brought the last of these dynasties, the Shutrukids, to an end at the close of the 12th century BC.

TROOP NOTES

The cities of lowland Susiana, of which Susa itself was the largest, were heavily influenced by Sumerian culture and it is likely that they had similar military systems to the city states of Mesopotamia. That these would include battle cars is shown by finds of models of such in graves from the region. It is probable that the influence existed through the later Isin-Larsa period as well. Whilst these city troops would only be available when Susania was not under the direct control of Mesopotamian powers, as happened regularly, the exact periods when this would occur are hard to define and so we do not attempt spurious accuracy by listing a series of speculative dates in the list.

From around the middle of the second millennium BC there are records showing that chariots were in use in the kingdom of Elam and Anshan and it is likely that development had followed that of the rest of the Middle East. After the end of the period covered by this list, Neo-Elamite armies fielded large numbers of distinctive "chariots" with a driver and up to 3 unarmoured archers on an open platform. It is uncertain whether these were used in the earlier period – we give the option to field chariots as Average to represent these.

EARLY ELAMITE STARTER ARMY (AFTER 1500 BC)		
Commander-in-Chief	1	Field Commander
Sub-commanders	2	2 x Troop Commander
Chariots	3 BGs	Each comprising 4 bases of chariots: Superior, Undrilled Light Chariots – Bow
Archers	8 BGs	Each comprising 6 bases of archers: Average, Unprotected, Undrilled Light Foot – Bow
Slingers	2 BGs	Each comprising 8 bases of slingers: Poor, Unprotected, Undrilled Light Foot – Sling
Camp	1	Unfortified camp
Total	13 BGs	Camp, 12 mounted bases, 64 foot bases, 3 commanders

BUILDING A CUSTOMISED LIST USING OUR ARMY POINTS

Choose an army based on the maxima and minima in the list below. The following special instructions apply to this army:

- Commanders should be depicted as archers, but also carrying an axe or sickle sword, or in a 4-wheeled battle car, 4- or 2- equid proto-chariot or 2-horse chariot if these are available for the army.

- An Elamite allied commander's contingent must conform to the Early Elamite allies list below, but the troops in the contingent are deducted from the minima and maxima in the main list.
- From 1500 BC only one Elamite allied commander can be used.

Archer

EARLY ELAMITE									
Territory Types: Agricultural, Hilly, Mountains									
C-in-C	Inspired Commander/Field Commander/Troop Commander						80/50/35	1	
Sub-commanders	Field Commander						50	0–2	
	Troop Commander						35		
Elamite allied commanders	Field Commander/Troop Commander						40/25	0–2	
Troop name	Troop Type				Capabilities		Points per base	Bases per BG	Total bases
	Type	Armour	Quality	Training	Shooting	Close Combat			
Core Troops									
Archers	Medium Foot	Unprotected	Average	Undrilled	Bow	–	5	6–8	24–200
			Poor				3		
	Light Foot	Unprotected	Average	Undrilled	Bow	–	5	6–8	
			Poor				3		
Slingers	Light Foot	Unprotected	Average	Undrilled	Sling	–	4	6–8	6–24
			Poor				2		

AMORITE KINGDOMS ALLIES

Allied commander		Field Commander/Troop Commander						40/25		1	
Troop name		Troop Type				Capabilities		Points per base	Bases per BG	Total bases	
		Type	Armour	Quality	Training	Shooting	Close Combat				
2-horse chariots	Only from 1800	Light Chariots	–	Superior	Undrilled	Bow	–	17	4	0–4	
Regular infantry		Medium Foot	Protected	Average	Drilled	–	Light Spear, Swordsmen	7	6–8	6–18	
Regular archers		Medium Foot	Unprotected	Average	Drilled	Bow	–	6	6–8	6–8	
Amorite levies		Medium Foot	Protected	Average	Undrilled	–	Light Spear, Swordsmen	6	6–8	6–24	
		Medium Foot	Protected	Average	Undrilled	–	Light Spear	5	6–8		
Archers		Light Foot	Unprotected	Average	Undrilled	Bow	–	5	6–8	0–8	6–24
				Poor				3			
Slingers		Light Foot	Unprotected	Average	Undrilled	Sling	–	4	6–8	0–12	
				Poor				2			
Javelinmen		Light Foot	Unprotected	Average	Undrilled	Javelins	Light Spear	4	6–8	6–16	
		Light Foot	Unprotected	Poor	Undrilled	Javelins	Light Spear	2	6–8	0–8	

VIETNAMESE

This list covers the armies of Vietnam from c.700 BC until 1009 AD. It can be used in themed tournaments based on Field of Glory Companion 11: *Empires of the Dragon*. It does not include those periods of Chinese domination, such as the Nanyue period (206–111 BC), when the country was effectively incorporated within a Chinese state, even if this state was not the dominant Imperial power.

Although there was a Vietnamese culture that dates back to the late third millennium BC, known to archaeologists as Phung-nguyen culture, it is not until the reign of the Chinese king Chuang of Zhou (696–682 BC) that there are true historical records of Vietnam. This period is known to archaeologists as the Dong-son culture, which lasted through to the first century AD and was Vietnam's Bronze Age. From at least the 4th century BC, Vietnam came under Chinese influence, to a greater or lesser degree depending on the situation within China itself, and at times was ruled by China or by regimes that were heavily Chinese influenced.

The earliest kingdom covered by this list is Van-lang, based around the Hong river delta, which was followed by Au Lac, ruled by the so called "Lac Lords". This was later dominated by China during the Qin and Han dynasties, which left Vietnam somewhat fractured between ruling clans.

Later powerful dynasties in Vietnam include the Early Ly dynasty, which was located in northern Vietnam near the Red River Delta from 544 to 603 AD. It was founded by Ly Bon and was regarded as a regional power with limited influence on other regions. The region also saw the Early Le dynasty founded by Le Hoan, established near Hanoi, which lasted from 980 to 1009 AD.

The allies list provides the Vietnamese allies referred to in Field of Glory Companion 11: *Empires of the Dragon*.

TROOP NOTES

Vietnamese warriors were armed with a variety of weapons, with spears and "boot-shaped" axes being typical. We classify these as Light Spear, Swordsmen.

The crossbow was introduced c.300 BC, and elephants c.250 AD.

VIETNAMESE STARTER ARMY (AFTER 250 AD)		
Commander-in-Chief	1	Field Commander
Sub-commanders	2	2 x Troop Commander
Elephants	1 BG	2 bases of elephants: Average, Undrilled Elephants
Warriors	5 BGs	Each comprising 8 bases of warriors: Average, Protected, Undrilled Medium Foot – Light Spear, Swordsmen
Crossbowmen	1 BG	8 bases of crossbowmen: Average, Unprotected, Undrilled Medium Foot – Crossbow
Archers	2 BGs	Each comprising 6 bases of archers: Average, Unprotected, Undrilled Medium Foot – Bow
Skirmishing archers	3 BGs	Each comprising 6 bases of skirmishing archers: Average, Unprotected, Undrilled Light Foot – Bow
Camp	1	Unfortified camp
Total	12 BGs	Camp, 2 mounted bases, 78 foot bases, 3 commanders

BUILDING A CUSTOMISED LIST USING OUR ARMY POINTS

Choose an army based on the maxima and minima in the list below. The following special instructions apply to this army:

- Commanders should be depicted as warriors or, after 250 AD, on elephants.

VIETNAMESE									
Territory Types: Hilly, Woodlands, Tropical									
C-in-C		Inspired Commander/Field Commander/Troop Commander					80/50/35		1
Sub-commanders		Field Commander					50		0–2
		Troop Commander					35		0–3
Troop name		Troop Type				Capabilities		Points per base	Bases per BG	Total bases
		Type	Armour	Quality	Training	Shooting	Close Combat			
Core Troops										
Warriors		Medium Foot	Protected	Average	Undrilled	–	Light Spear, Swordsmen	6	6–10	18–100
Archers or crossbowmen	Any date	Medium Foot	Unprotected	Average	Undrilled	Bow	–	5	6–8	12–60
	Only from 300 BC	Medium Foot	Unprotected	Average	Undrilled	Crossbow	–	5	6–8	
Skirmishing archers or crossbowmen	Any date	Light Foot	Unprotected	Average	Undrilled	Bow	–	5	6–8	6–24
	Only from 300 BC	Light Foot	Unprotected	Average	Undrilled	Crossbow	–	5	6–8	
Optional Troops										
Javelinmen		Light Foot	Unprotected	Average	Undrilled	Javelins	Light Spear	4	6–8	0–18
Subject or poor quality warriors		Medium Foot	Protected	Average	Undrilled	–	Light Spear	5	6–10	0–24
				Poor				3		
Subject or poor quality archers		Medium Foot	Unprotected	Average	Undrilled	Bow	–	5	6–8	0–12
				Poor				3		
		Light Foot	Unprotected	Average	Undrilled	Bow	–	5	6–8	
				Poor				3		
Elephants	Only from 250 AD	Elephants	–	Average	Undrilled	–	–	25	2	0–2
Levy or other peasants		Mob	Unprotected	Poor	Undrilled	–	–	2	10–12	0–24

VIETNAMESE ALLIES

C-in-C		Inspired Commander/Field Commander/Troop Commander						80/50/35		1
Troop name		**Troop Type**				**Capabilities**		**Points per base**	**Bases per BG**	**Total bases**
		Type	Armour	Quality	Training	Shooting	Close Combat			
Warriors		Medium Foot	Protected	Average	Undrilled	–	Light Spear, Swordsmen	6	6–10	6–30
Archers or crossbowmen	Any date	Medium Foot	Unprotected	Average	Undrilled	Bow	–	5	6–8	6–24
	Only from 300 BC	Medium Foot	Unprotected	Average	Undrilled	Crossbow	–	5	6–8	
Skirmishing archers or crossbowmen	Any date	Light Foot	Unprotected	Average	Undrilled	Bow	–	5	6–8	6–8
	Only from 300 BC	Light Foot	Unprotected	Average	Undrilled	Crossbow	–	5	6–8	

PRE-ISLAMIC ARABIAN

This list covers the southern pre-Islamic and apostate armies of the Arabian peninsula from c.300 AD until the final adoption of Islam by the whole of the peninsula at the end of the Ridda Wars. It can be used in themed tournaments based on Field of Glory Companion 5: *Legions Triumphant* or Field of Glory Companion 7: *Decline and Fall*.

The southern part of the Arabian peninsula, modern Yemen, Oman and the United Arab Emirates, was ruled by a number of Sabaean-Himyaritic kingdoms based on settled agriculture rather than the nomadic/semi-nomadic culture of much of the rest of Arabia. Judaism, and to a much lesser extent Christianity, were common in the region amongst both rulers and ruled, in addition to traditional Arab paganism.

Foot Warrior

TROOP NOTES

The Sassanids sent a number of small expeditions to south Arabia to assist in expelling the Christian Axumites who were, of course, allies of the Byzantines and so enemies of Persia. Additionally, control of the valuable Red Sea trade routes was a factor, and from 598 AD a formal Persian satrapy was formed, ending when the last satrap converted to Islam. Few troops appear to have been sent, but they included a body of infantry who were either Dailami or freed prisoners depending on which account you believe. Dailami is possibly more likely as later accounts record the name "al-Daylam" in the area. The presence of significant numbers of Persian cavalry is uncertain but we have given the benefit of the doubt.

Accounts of fighting in the Ridda Wars suggest that south Arabian troops were essentially the same as their Muslim opponents. Some Bedouin were employed to guard the desert fringes, but large scale contingents were supplied through alliances.

PRE–ISLAMIC ARABIAN STARTER ARMY

Commander-in-Chief	1	Field Commander
Sub-commanders	2	2 x Troop Commander
City cavalry	1 BG	4 bases of city cavalry: Superior, Armoured, Undrilled Cavalry – Lancers, Swordsmen
Bedouin cavalry	2 BGs	Each comprising 4 bases of Bedouin cavalry: Average, Unprotected, Undrilled Light Horse – Lancers, Swordsmen
Camel-mounted scouts	1 BG	4 bases of camel-mounted scouts: Average, Unprotected, Undrilled Camelry – Bow
Foot warriors	4 BGs	Each comprising 6 bases of foot warriors: Average, Protected, Undrilled Heavy Foot – Light Spear, Swordsmen and 3 bases of supporting archers: Average, Unprotected, Undrilled Light Foot – Bow
Separately deployed archers	2 BGs	Each comprising 6 bases of separately deployed archers: Average, Unprotected, Undrilled Light Foot – Bow
Slingers	1 BG	6 bases of slingers: Average, Unprotected, Undrilled Light Foot – Sling
Javelinmen	1 BG	6 bases of javelinmen: Average, Unprotected, Undrilled Light Foot – Javelins, Light Spear
Camp	1	Unfortified camp
Total	12 BGs	Camp, 16 mounted bases, 60 foot bases, 3 commanders

BUILDING A CUSTOMISED LIST USING OUR ARMY POINTS

Choose an army based on the maxima and minima in the list below. The following special instructions apply to this army:

- Commanders should be depicted as foot warriors, Bedouin cavalry, city cavalry or, from 570 to 628, as Sassanid cavalry.
- The minimum marked * only applies if Sassanid cavalry are used.

PRE–ISLAMIC ARABIAN

Territory Types: Agricultural, Steppes

C-in-C	Inspired Commander/Field Commander/Troop Commander				80/50/35		1	
Sub-commanders	Field Commander				50		0–2	
	Troop Commander				35		0–3	

Troop name	Troop Type				Capabilities		Points per base	Bases per BG	Total bases
	Type	Armour	Quality	Training	Shooting	Close Combat			
Core Troops									
City cavalry	Cavalry	Armoured	Superior	Undrilled	–	Lancers, Swordsmen	16	4–6	0–6
		Armoured	Average				12		
		Protected	Superior				12		
		Protected	Average				9		
Foot warriors	Heavy Foot	Protected	Average	Undrilled	–	Light Spear, Swordsmen	6	2/3 or all	24–120
Supporting archers	Light Foot	Unprotected	Average	Undrilled	Bow	–	5	1/3 or 0	0–24
Separately deployed archers	Medium Foot	Protected	Average	Undrilled	Bow	–	6	6–8	0–24
	Light Foot	Unprotected	Average	Undrilled	Bow	–	5	6–8	0–12

Optional Troops									
Bedouin cavalry	Light Horse	Unprotected	Average	Undrilled	–	Lancers, Swordsmen	8	4–6	0–8
	Cavalry	Unprotected	Average	Undrilled	–	Lancers, Swordsmen	8	4–6	
		Protected					9		
Camel-mounted scouts	Camelry	Unprotected	Average	Undrilled	Bow	–	10	4	0–4
Slingers	Light Foot	Unprotected	Average	Undrilled	Sling	–	4	4–6	0–6
Javelinmen	Medium Foot	Protected	Average	Undrilled	–	Light Spear	5	6–8	0–16
	Light Foot	Unprotected	Average	Undrilled	Javelins	Light Spear	4	6–8	
Fortified camp							24		0–1
Allies									
Bedouin allies (up to 2 contingents) – Later Pre-Islamic Bedouin									
Special Campaigns									
Only from 570 to 628									
Dailami or freed prisoners	Medium Foot	Protected	Superior	Undrilled	–	Impact Foot, Swordsmen	9	4–6	*4–6
	Medium Foot	Protected	Average	Undrilled	–	Light Spear	5	4–6	
Sassanid cavalry	Cavalry	Armoured	Superior	Undrilled	Bow	Swordsmen	18	4	0–4

PRE-ISLAMIC ARABIAN ALLIES

Allied commander	Field Commander/Troop Commander						40/25		1
Troop name	Troop Type				Capabilities		Points per base	Bases per BG	Total bases
	Type	Armour	Quality	Training	Shooting	Close Combat			
City cavalry	Cavalry	Armoured	Superior	Undrilled	–	Lancers, Swordsmen	16	4	0–4
		Armoured	Average				12		
		Protected	Superior				12		
		Protected	Average				9		
Bedouin cavalry	Light Horse	Unprotected	Average	Undrilled	–	Lancers, Swordsmen	8	4	0–4
	Cavalry	Unprotected	Average	Undrilled	–	Lancers, Swordsmen	8	4	
		Protected					9		
Foot warriors	Heavy Foot	Protected	Average	Undrilled	–	Light Spear, Swordsmen	6	2/3 or all	8–32
Supporting archers	Light Foot	Unprotected	Average	Undrilled	Bow	–	5	1/3 or 0	0–8
Separately deployed archers	Medium Foot	Protected	Average	Undrilled	Bow	–	6	4	0–4
	Light Foot	Unprotected	Average	Undrilled	Bow	–	5	4	
Javelinmen	Medium Foot	Protected	Average	Undrilled	–	Light Spear	5	4–6	0–6
	Light Foot	Unprotected	Average	Undrilled	Javelins	Light Spear	4	4–6	

LATER PRE-ISLAMIC BEDOUIN

From the late 4th century AD onwards both the Romans and Sassanid Persians placed increased reliance on allied Arab tribes to guard their desert frontiers against other raiding Arabs. During the 5th century this reliance was increased, possibly as a result of both empires needing to concentrate their resources to fight barbarians on other fronts. As a result, large federations of Arab tribes evolved

under the aegis of imperial patronage. In addition to their role in controlling other Arabs, they also began to undertake significant military operations both by themselves and in conjunction with their imperial masters.

This list covers Bedouin armies of the Salih and their successors the Ghassanids, allied to the Romans, from c.420 to 636, and the Lakhmids, based around the city of al-Hirah, allied to the Persians, from c.400 to 602. It can be used in themed tournaments based on Field of Glory Companion 5: *Legions Triumphant* or Field of Glory Companion 7: *Decline and Fall*.

It also provides an allied contingent for armies with Bedouin allies in the Arabian peninsula and can be used by Roman and Sassanid armies during the periods noted above instead of the Early Arab allies list.

TROOP NOTES

One Lakhmid leader is reported to have had 300 mail shirts which were distributed to the most valiant warriors in his army prior to a battle with the Sassanids. As the major tribal confederations were supplied with such gifts by Rome and Persia it is likely that similar equipment would be available to confederations other than the Lakhmids.

Additionally, the Lakhmids are recorded as having a regiment of Persian cavalry, the al-Shahba, provided by the Sassanid king. It was stationed at their capital, al-Hirah.

Although the desired mount for war was the horse, there are accounts of some camel riders in Bedouin armies, but they were clearly seen as inferior to the horse-mounted warrior. These camel riders are especially likely in allied contingents from camel herding nomads from the deep desert regions.

Bedouin Cavalryman

LAKHMID STARTER ARMY		
Commander-in-Chief	1	Troop Commander
Sub-commanders	2	2 x Troop Commander
Armoured cavalry	1 BG	4 bases of armoured cavalry: Superior, Armoured, Undrilled Cavalry – Lancers, Swordsmen
Al-Shahba Sassanid cavalry	1 BG	4 bases of Sassanid cavalry: Superior, Armoured, Undrilled Cavalry – Bow, Swordsmen
Bedouin cavalry	4 BGs	Each comprising 4 bases of Bedouin cavalry: Average, Protected, Undrilled Cavalry – Lancers, Swordsmen
Bedouin cavalry	4 BGs	Each comprising 4 bases of Bedouin cavalry: Average, Unprotected, Undrilled Light Horse – Lancers, Swordsmen
Archers	1 BG	6 bases of archers: Average, Unprotected, Undrilled Light Foot – Bow
Slingers	1 BG	6 bases of slingers: Average, Unprotected, Undrilled Light Foot – Sling
Javelinmen	1 BG	8 bases of javelinmen: Average, Unprotected, Undrilled Light Foot – Javelins, Light Spear
Camp	1	Unfortified camp
Total	13 BGs	Camp, 40 mounted bases, 20 foot bases, 3 commanders

BUILDING A CUSTOMISED LIST USING OUR ARMY POINTS

Choose an army based on the maxima and minima in the list below. The following special instructions apply to this army:

- Commanders should be depicted as Bedouin cavalry or Armoured cavalry.

- A Later Pre-Islamic Bedouin allied commander's contingent must conform to the Later Pre-Islamic Bedouin Allies list below, but the troops in the contingent are deducted from the minima and maxima in the main list.
- Al-Shahba cavalry cannot be used with camel riders.

LATER PRE-ISLAMIC BEDOUIN

Territory Types: Only Lakhmids – Agricultural, Steppes, Desert. Others – Steppes, Desert.

C-in-C	Inspired Commander/Field Commander/Troop Commander					80/50/35		1
Sub-commanders	Field Commander					50		0–2
	Troop Commander					35		
Later Bedouin allied commanders	Field Commander/Troop Commander					40/25		0–2

Troop name	Troop Type				Capabilities		Points per base	Bases per BG	Total bases
	Type	Armour	Quality	Training	Shooting	Close Combat			
Core Troops									
Bedouin cavalry	Light Horse	Unprotected	Average	Undrilled	–	Lancers, Swordsmen	8	4–6	24–120
	Cavalry	Unprotected	Average	Undrilled	–	Lancers, Swordsmen	8	4–6	
		Protected					9		
Optional Troops									
Armoured cavalry	Cavalry	Armoured	Superior	Undrilled	–	Lancers, Swordsmen	16	4	0–4
			Average				12		
Al-Shahba Sassanid cavalry	Only Lakhmids	Cavalry	Armoured	Superior	Undrilled	Bow	Swordsmen	18	4	0–4
Camel riders	Camelry	Unprotected	Average	Undrilled	–	Light Spear	9	4–6	0–8	0–8
	Camelry	Unprotected	Average	Undrilled	Bow	–	10	4	0–4	
Archers	Light Foot	Unprotected	Average	Undrilled	Bow	–	5	6–8	0–12	0–12
Slingers	Light Foot	Unprotected	Average	Undrilled	Sling	–	4	6–8	0–8	
Javelinmen	Light Foot	Unprotected	Average	Undrilled	Javelins	Light Spear	4	6–8	0–12
	Medium Foot	Protected	Average	Undrilled	–	Light Spear, Swordsmen	6	6–8	

LATER PRE-ISLAMIC BEDOUIN ALLIES

Allied commander	Field Commander/Troop Commander					40/25		1

Troop name	Troop Type				Capabilities		Points per base	Bases per BG	Total bases
	Type	Armour	Quality	Training	Shooting	Close Combat			
Bedouin cavalry	Light Horse	Unprotected	Average	Undrilled	–	Lancers, Swordsmen	8	4–6	4–30
	Cavalry	Unprotected	Average	Undrilled	–	Lancers, Swordsmen	8	4–6	
		Protected					9		
Camel riders	Camelry	Unprotected	Average	Undrilled	–	Light Spear	9	4–6	0–8	0–8
	Camelry	Unprotected	Average	Undrilled	Bow	–	10	4	0–4	

AXUMITE

This list covers Axumite armies from 100 to 970 AD. It can be used in themed tournaments based on Field of Glory Companion 7: *Decline and Fall*.

Axum emerged in the 1st century AD on the highland plateau of what is now Eritrea and Tigray. At the height of its power, in the 4th to 6th centuries AD, it dominated the region and controlled the profitable trade through the Red Sea from south Asia to the Mediterranean.

Axum had a rich culture characterised by distinctive architecture, well developed agriculture, its own coinage and written records in Greek and its native Ge'ez. The kingdom followed pagan gods until the official adoption of Christianity from the 4th century.

At its greatest extent, Axum's dominion included the former Nile Valley kingdom of Meroe, the Red Sea coast from Egypt to Somalia and, at various times, parts of the Arabian coast, south-west Arabia, as well as much of the Ethiopian highlands. Ezana in the mid-4th century was Axum's foremost conqueror and became the first Axumite king to convert to Christianity.

Diplomatic links were well established with the Byzantine Empire, which supported the Axumite King Kaleb in the early 6th century for a major military expedition to the Himyar Kingdom in south-west Arabia. With the rise of Islam in the 7th century, Axum became effectively isolated and lost control of the lucrative Red Sea trade. Its gradual decline continued from then until the late 10th century.

TROOP NOTES

The Axumite army was organised into regiments (*sarawit*) of unknown size, each with its own regional, tribal or possibly functional name. It is probable that most of these were levy troops although there was probably a small professional guard or core as in later medieval Ethiopia.

Most soldiers fought on foot with javelins and spears, which could be short or long bladed. Ethiopians were famed for their use of these and also fought as mercenaries from North Africa to Persia. Broadswords were also used and depicted as worn slung on the back. Other weapons included bows and knives. Round shields were probably in common use but other personal armour was likely to be rare. Horses were valued possessions and probably not as common in warfare as in later periods. The extent to which elephants were used in war is not known. A failed Axumite military attack on Mecca in 570 is known in Arabic sources as the Year of the Elephant after their use in the battle by the Axumites. Kaleb's ceremonial chariot was drawn by four elephants. Camels were used in desert warfare by Beja and Noba allies but probably more commonly used as transport.

Axumite governor, Yemeni guard and Omani marine, by Angus McBride. Taken from Men-At-Arms 243: Rome's Enemies (5): The Desert Frontier.

AXUMITE STARTER ARMY

Commander-in-Chief	1	Field Commander
Sub-commanders	2	2 x Troop Commander
Cavalry	2 BGs	Each comprising 4 bases of cavalry: Average, Unprotected, Undrilled Light Horse – Javelins, Light Spear
Veteran spearmen	2 BGs	Each comprising 8 bases of veteran spearmen: Superior, Protected, Undrilled Medium Foot – Impact Foot, Swordsmen
Other spearmen	3 BGs	Each comprising 8 bases of other spearmen: Average, Protected, Undrilled Medium Foot – Impact Foot, Swordsmen
Elephants	1 BG	2 bases of elephants: Average Undrilled Elephants
Archers	2 BGs	Each comprising 6 bases of archers: Average, Unprotected, Undrilled Light Foot – Bow
Camp	1	Unfortified camp
Total	10 BGs	Camp, 10 mounted bases, 52 foot bases, 3 commanders

BUILDING A CUSTOMISED LIST USING OUR ARMY POINTS

Choose an army based on the maxima and minima in the list below. The following special instructions apply to this army:

- Commanders should be depicted as cavalry or elephants.
- Pre-Islamic Arabian or Later Pre-Islamic Bedouin allies cannot be used with Blemmye or Meroitic allies.

AXUMITE

Territory Types: Agricultural, Hilly, Desert.

C-in-C		Inspired Commander/Field Commander/Troop Commander				80/50/35		1	
Sub-commanders		Field Commander				50		0–2	
		Troop Commander				35		0–3	
Troop name	Troop Type				Capabilities		Points per base	Bases per BG	Total bases
	Type	Armour	Quality	Training	Shooting	Close Combat			
Core Troops									
Cavalry	Light Horse	Unprotected	Average	Undrilled	Javelins	Light Spear	7	4–6	4–8
Veteran or guard spearmen	Medium Foot	Protected	Superior	Undrilled	–	Impact Foot, Swordsmen	9	6–8	0–16 / 24–120
Other spearmen	Medium Foot	Protected	Average	Undrilled	–	Impact Foot, Swordsmen	7	8–12	24–120
Archers	Light Foot	Unprotected	Average	Undrilled	Bow	–	5	6–8	6–32
	Medium Foot	Unprotected	Average	Undrilled	Bow	–	5	6–8	
Optional Troops									
Elephants	Elephants	–	Average	Undrilled	–	–	25	2	0–2
Skirmishing javelinmen	Light Foot	Unprotected	Average	Undrilled	Javelins	Light Spear	4	6–8	0–8
Allies									
Beja (desert Blemmye) allies – Beja, Nile valley Blemmye or Early Nobatae									
Meroitic allies									
Pre-Islamic Arabian allies									
Later Pre-Islamic Bedouin allies									

MEROITIC ALLIES

Allied commander	Field Commander/Troop Commander						40/25		1	
Troop name	Troop Type				Capabilities		Points per base	Bases per BG	Total bases	
	Type	Armour	Quality	Training	Shooting	Close Combat				
Cavalry	Cavalry	Protected	Average	Undrilled	—	Light Spear, Swordsmen	9	4–6	0–6	
		Unprotected					8			
	Light Horse	Unprotected	Average	Undrilled	Javelins	Light Spear	7	4–6		
Archers	Medium Foot	Unprotected	Average	Undrilled	Bow	—	5	6–8	8–24	
			Poor				3			
	Light Foot	Unprotected	Average	Undrilled	Bow	—	5	6–8		
			Poor				3			
Spearmen	Medium Foot	Protected	Poor	Undrilled	—	Defensive Spearmen	4	6–8	6–36	

BEJA, NILE VALLEY BLEMMYE OR EARLY NOBATAE

This list covers Beja (desert Blemmye) forces from 250 to 1500 AD, and Nile valley Blemmye or Nobatae forces from 298 to 550 AD. It can be used in themed tournaments based on Field of Glory Companion 5: *Legions Triumphant* or Field of Glory Companion 7: *Decline and Fall*.

The Blemmye were a nomadic people living in the desert between the Nile and the Red Sea from at least the 1st century BC. They began to raid Roman Egypt in the 3rd century AD. The Nobatae were a similar people living to the west of the Nile.

In 298 AD the Emperor Diocletian withdrew Roman forces from Nubia. The Blemmye established control over the north of Lower Nubia, while the Nobatae controlled the south.

In the mid-6th century, the Blemmye were driven back into the desert by the Nobatae, who adopted Christianity under Byzantine influence. Later Nobatian armies are covered by the Christian Nubian list in Field of Glory Companion 7: *Decline and Fall*.

The desert Blemmye were later called Beja. We designate them thus throughout the list for the sake of clarity.

TROOP NOTES

Beja camel-mounted warriors fighting for the Christian Nubian states are described as poorly armoured or naked and fighting with spears. They were routed with ease by Arab cavalry who, on one occasion, tied bells to their horses to frighten the camels.

From about the middle of the 9th century the Beja came under increasing Arab influence eventually becoming at least nominally Muslim. It is likely that this influence resulted in a greater use of cavalry along Arab lines, although their equipment levels would still be much lower.

In the 6th century some Nile valley Blemmye or Nobatae cavalry may have been equipped with bows under Byzantine influence.

BEJA STARTER ARMY (AFTER 850 AD)

Commander-in-Chief	1	Troop Commander
Sub-commanders	2	2 x Troop Commander
Camelry	6 BGs	Each comprising 4 bases of camelry: Average, Protected, Undrilled Camelry – Light Spear
Cavalry	4 BGs	Each comprising 4 bases of cavalry: Average, Unprotected, Undrilled Light Horse – Lancers, Swordsmen
Archers	5 BGs	Each comprising 6 bases of archers: Average, Unprotected, Undrilled Light Foot – Bow
Camp	1	Unfortified camp
Total	15 BGs	Camp, 40 mounted bases, 30 foot bases, 3 commanders

BUILDING A CUSTOMISED LIST USING OUR ARMY POINTS

Choose an army based on the maxima and minima in the list below. The following special instructions apply to this army:

- Beja commanders should be depicted as camelry or cavalry. Nile Valley Blemmye or Nobatae commanders should be depicted as cavalry.

- An army must be Beja, Nile valley Blemmye or Nobatae.

- Date restrictions specified for "Nile valley Blemmye or Nobatae" apply to both.

BEJA, NILE VALLEY BLEMMYE OR EARLY NOBATAE

Territory Types: Only Beja – Desert, Hilly. Only Nile valley Blemmye or Nobatae – Agricultural, Hilly.

C-in-C			Inspired Commander/Field Commander/Troop Commander						80/50/35		1
Sub-commanders			Field Commander						50		0–2
			Troop Commander						35		0–3
Troop name			Troop Type				Capabilities		Points per base	Bases per BG	Total bases
			Type	Armour	Quality	Training	Shooting	Close Combat			
Core Troops											
Cavalry	Only Beja before 850		Light Horse	Unprotected	Average	Undrilled	Javelins	Light Spear	7	4–6	0–8
			Cavalry	Unprotected	Average	Undrilled	–	Light Spear, Swordsmen	8	4–6	
				Protected					9		
	Only Beja from 850		Light Horse	Unprotected	Average	Undrilled	–	Lancers, Swordsmen	8	4–6	0–18
			Cavalry	Unprotected	Average	Undrilled	–	Lancers, Swordsmen	8	4–6	
				Protected					9		
	Only Nile valley Blemmye or Nobatae from 298 to 550		Light Horse	Unprotected	Average	Undrilled	Javelins	Light Spear	7	4–6	8–30
			Cavalry	Unprotected	Average	Undrilled	–	Light Spear, Swordsmen	8	4–6	
				Protected					9		
			Cavalry	Armoured	Superior	Undrilled	–	Light Spear, Swordsmen	16	4–6	
				Protected					12		
	Only Nile valley Blemmye or Nobatae from 500		Cavalry	Armoured	Superior	Undrilled	Bow*	Light Spear, Swordsmen	18	4–6	0–6
				Protected					14		
Camelry			Camelry	Protected	Average	Undrilled	–	Light Spear	9	4–6	Beja 24–76, Others 0–16
				Protected	Poor				7		
				Unprotected	Average				8		
				Unprotected	Poor				6		

56

Foot warriors		Medium Foot	Protected	Average	Undrilled	–	Light Spear	5	8–12	0–32
Archers		Medium Foot	Unprotected	Average	Undrilled	Bow	–	5	6–8	Beja 0–48, Others 12–148
		Light Foot	Unprotected	Average	Undrilled	Bow	–	5	6–8	
Kushite spearmen	Only Nile valley Blemmye or Nobatae	Medium Foot	Protected	Poor	Undrilled	–	Defensive Spearmen	4	8–12	10–48
Allies										
Beja allies										

BEJA ALLIES

Allied commander	Field Commander/Troop Commander						40/25		1	
Troop name	**Troop Type**				**Capabilities**		**Points per base**	**Bases per BG**	**Total bases**	
	Type	Armour	Quality	Training	Shooting	Close Combat				
Camelry	Camelry	Protected	Average	Undrilled	–	Light Spear	9	4–6	8–24	
		Protected	Poor				7			
		Unprotected	Average	Undrilled	–	Light Spear	8			
		Unprotected	Poor				6			
Archers	Light Foot	Unprotected	Average	Undrilled	Bow	–	5	6–8	0–16	
	Medium Foot	Unprotected	Average	Undrilled	Bow	–	5	6–8		
Foot warriors	Medium Foot	Protected	Average	Undrilled	–	Light Spear	5	8–10	0–10	

TUAREG

This list covers Tuareg and similar western desert tribe armies from 950 to 1500 AD.

Battles involving desert tribes using massed camelry go back as far as the latter 10th century in sub-Saharan Africa. At various times Tuareg and other desert tribes fought against or allied themselves with Songhay, Hausa and Bornu.

TROOP NOTES

Most of the evidence comes from later periods, but there is no reason to suppose that earlier Tuareg fighting styles differed significantly.

Camelry represent the Ihaggaren nobles and their mounted Imrad vassals. Weapons were the *allarh*, a short lance made entirely of iron, javelins,

sword and shield. Other Imrad fought on foot. Iklan were black servants or serfs.

Cavalry were used in later periods when the Tuaregs controlled territory capable of supporting them, and may have been used in this period.

Tuareg Camelry

TUAREG STARTER ARMY		
Commander-in-Chief	1	Field Commander
Sub-commanders	2	2 x Troop Commander
Camelry	6 BGs	Each comprising 4 bases of camelry: Superior, Protected, Undrilled Camelry – Lancers, Swordsmen
Imrad foot	2 BGs	Each comprising 8 bases of Imrad foot: Average, Protected, Undrilled Medium Foot – Impact Foot, Swordsmen
Iklan levies	2 BGs	Each comprising 8 bases of Iklan levies: Poor, Unprotected, Drilled Light Foot – Javelins, Light Spear
Camp	1	Unfortified camp
Total	10 BGs	Camp, 24 mounted bases, 32 foot bases, 3 commanders

BUILDING A CUSTOMISED LIST USING OUR ARMY POINTS

Choose an army based on the maxima and minima in the list below. The following special instructions apply to this army:

- Commanders should be depicted as camelry or cavalry.
- A Tuareg allied commander's contingent must conform to the Tuareg allies list below, but the troops in the contingent are deducted from the minima and maxima in the main list.
- Camelry and cavalry can only dismount when permitted to do so by the standard rules. When they do so, they dismount as Medium Foot, Protected, Superior or Average (as mounted type), Undrilled, Impact Foot, Swordsmen.

TUAREG								
Territory Types: Desert, Hilly								
C-in-C	Inspired Commander/Field Commander/Troop Commander					80/50/35		1
Sub-commanders	Field Commander					50		0–2
	Troop Commander					35		0–3
Tuareg allied commanders	Field Commander/Troop Commander					40/25		0–2
Troop name	Troop Type				Capabilities		Points per base	Bases per BG	Total bases
	Type	Armour	Quality	Training	Shooting	Close Combat			
Core Troops									
Camelry	Camelry	Protected	Superior	Undrilled	–	Lancers, Swordsmen	14	4–6	16–54
			Average				11		
Imrad or mountain tribe foot	Medium Foot	Protected	Average	Undrilled	–	Impact Foot, Swordsmen	7	8–12	0–32
Iklan levies	Light Foot	Unprotected	Poor	Undrilled	Javelins	Light Spear	2	6–8	0–16 / 0–24
	Medium Foot	Protected	Poor	Undrilled	–	Light Spear	3	6–8	0–16
Optional Troops									
Cavalry	Cavalry	Protected	Superior	Undrilled	–	Lancers, Swordsmen	12	4–6	0–12
			Average				9		

TUAREG ALLIES

Allied commander	Field Commander/Troop Commander						40/25		1
Troop name	**Troop Type**			**Capabilities**			**Points per base**	**Bases per BG**	**Total bases**
	Type	Armour	Quality	Training	Shooting	Close Combat			
Camelry	Camelry	Protected	Superior	Undrilled	–	Lancers, Swordsmen	14	4–6	4–16
			Average				11		
Imrad or mountain tribe foot	Medium Foot	Protected	Average	Undrilled	–	Impact Foot, Swordsmen	7	8–12	0–12
Iklan levies	Light Foot	Unprotected	Poor	Undrilled	Javelins	Light Spear	2	6–8	0–8
	Medium Foot	Protected	Poor	Undrilled	–	Light Spear	3	6–8	
Cavalry	Cavalry	Protected	Superior	Undrilled	–	Lancers, Swordsmen	12	4	0–4
			Average				9		

MEDIEVAL GERMAN CITY LEAGUES

This list covers the armies of the various city leagues (Hanseatic League, 1st and 2nd Swabian League, Lusatian League), and those of some of the more powerful cities, from 1300 to 1500 AD. It can be used in themed tournaments based on Field of Glory Companion 2: *Storm of Arrows.*

City leagues were founded for various reasons, sometimes mainly to further commercial aims – like the Hanseatic League. Others, like the 2nd Swabian League (Schwäbischer Bund), were an attempt to bring together various powerful groups in the hope of stopping or at least limiting the incessant wars in Germany. Most were simply alliances for mutual protection from aggressors and to protect the countryside from robbers (often local nobility).

Of those leagues, the Hanse is probably the most famous and longest lasting. It included not only independent cities but also other groups, including the Teutonic Order. At the height of its power, in the 14th century, it even waged wars with a powerful country like Denmark and eventually won out. Various political

Crossbowman

changes eventually led the Hanse into decline during the 15th century. In 1441, after losing the Dutch–Hanseatic war, the Hanse lost its quasi-monopoly on Baltic trade and had to recognize the Low Country cities as equals. In 1474 it won the (almost exclusively naval) Anglo–Hanse war, receiving trade privileges and ownership over the Stahlhof (Steelyard) area in London. Even in decline, the Hanse remained a power to be reckoned with well into the 16th century, and was never officially dissolved, although the last Hanse meeting was held in 1669.

The 1st Swabian League was founded in 1331. It soon began to include some nobles and rose in power. This caused a counter-reaction from several lesser nobles, who joined together, forming a knightly league called Schleglerbund. The Swabian League was defeated and dissolved by Graf Eberhard II von Württemberg in 1372. It reformed in 1376, which prompted several more battles between the League and the House of Württemberg. The net effect of those battles was a stalemate that preserved the independence of the League cities.

Rising tension between these leagues led to civil war in 1367. The Emperor, jealous of the growing power of the cities, endeavoured to set

Mounted crossbowman, German knight and pikeman, by Angus McBride.
Taken from Men-At-Arms 166: German Medieval Armies 1300–1500.

up a league under his own control. The defeat of the city league by Eberhard II, Count of Württemberg in 1372, the murder of the captain of the league, and the breach of his obligations by Karl IV, led to the formation of a new league of 14 Swabian cities led by Ulm in 1376. This league triumphed over the count of Württemberg at Reutlingen in 1377, and, the Emperor lifting his ban on the league, set up an arbitration court. Afterwards the league rapidly extended over Bavaria and Franconia, and finally fused with the Rhenish League. Württemberg struck back,

however, and defeated the league in 1388 at the Battle of Döffingen. King Wenzel then coerced all sides to accept a *Landfrieden* (treaty of public peace), which in effect meant dissolving all city and knightly leagues.

The 2nd Swabian League was somewhat unique amongst the city leagues as it was founded on the behalf of the Emperor. It not only included several powerful nobles and a knightly league (St. Georgschild) but even succeeded in incorporating these feudal elements into an effective command structure. It was the main source of troops in the Swabian war with the Swiss. It is more well known, however, for its assistance in the suppression of the Peasants' Revolt (1524–25).

TROOP NOTES

The free cities usually lacked adequate numbers of knights owing them service. Some resorted to deals with local nobles, gaining the service of a few knights in time of need. The larger leagues sometimes included feudal elements, providing them with much needed knights. These were usually supplemented by (and sometimes completely replaced by) mercenaries. Nevertheless, most city armies had a somewhat low ratio of men-at-arms to infantry. Whether mercenary men-at-arms were less bold or more disciplined than feudal ones is open to doubt, as they were often nobles themselves.

Konstaflers are urban knights, rich burghers and their followers. While generally well equipped, they were often lacking in training and were rarely willing to take any risks.

Lighter men-at-arms are basically knights who could not afford the full armour panoply of the time, resorting to refurbished older armours and forgoing horse barding. Initially they were deployed in the rear ranks of normal knight formations. Over time they were increasingly moved into separate units to make use of the higher mobility they could achieve. This led to them taking on a different tactical role, acting as the vanguard or rearguard of an army, as out-flankers or to protect flanks. In pitched battles they often dismounted to fight.

Halberdiers and *bidenhänder* (two-handed sword) wielders were most common in south Germany, were they were sometimes employed in small groups that moved around the spearmen (or later pikemen) to get at the flank of enemies frontally engaged.

Verlorene Haufen (forlorn hope) could be used as one large group to engage the enemy while the main army advanced, but were more often employed in small groups to disrupt enemy formations through their impact (or just as often by making the enemy pursue) or as rearguards if the army retreated.

Fußknechte were followers armed with a miscellany of weapons, mostly short spears, morningstars, warflails, clubs and swords. We treat this mixture as equivalent to Swordsmen capability.

Hanse marines were mercenaries employed by the Hanse cities mainly to be used in naval combat. They could also be deployed on land, however. While they are described as well trained and equipped we assume that they were not used to operating in large bodies, hence class them as Undrilled. Also it seems likely that they used smaller shields, as customary for ship-to-ship battles. The armoured option is provided under the assumption that they may have used larger shields while fighting on land.

Italian mercenary infantry and *Geldrische knechte* in the Swabian Wars are assumed to be taken from the infantry available in the main list.

MEDIEVAL GERMAN CITY LEAGUE STARTER ARMY (AFTER 1488 AD)		
Commander-in-Chief	1	Field Commander
Sub-commanders	2	2 x Troop Commander
Feudal or mercenary men-at-arms	1 BG	4 bases of men-at-arms: Superior, Heavily Armoured, Undrilled Knights – Lancers, Swordsmen
Mounted crossbowmen	1 BG	4 bases of mounted crossbowmen: Average, Armoured, Drilled Cavalry – Crossbow, Swordsmen
Halberdiers	1 BG	6 bases of halberdiers: Average, Armoured, Drilled Heavy Foot – Heavy Weapon
Landsknecht pikemen	3 BGs	Each comprising 8 bases of Landsknecht pikemen: Average, Protected, Drilled Heavy Foot – Pikemen
Militia or mercenary crossbowmen	2 BGs	Each comprising 6 bases of militia or mercenary crossbowmen: Average, Protected, Drilled Medium Foot – Crossbow
Handgunners	2 BGs	Each comprising 4 bases of handgunners: Average, Protected, Drilled Light Foot – Firearm
Camp	1	Unfortified camp
Total	10 BGs	Camp, 8 mounted bases, 50 foot bases, 3 commanders

BUILDING A CUSTOMISED LIST USING OUR ARMY POINTS

Choose an army based on the maxima and minima in the list below. The following special instructions apply to this army:

- Commanders should be depicted as knights.
- Feudal or mercenary men-at-arms can always dismount as Superior or Average (as mounted type), Heavily Armoured, Undrilled or Drilled (as mounted type), Heavy Foot – Heavy Weapon.
- Lighter Men-at-Arms can always dismount as Average, Armoured, Undrilled or Drilled (as mounted type), Heavy Foot – Heavy Weapon.
- *Konstaflers* can always dismount as Average, Heavily Armoured, Undrilled, Heavy Foot – Heavy Weapon.
- *Fußknechte* can be graded as Heavy Foot or Medium Foot but all must be graded the same.
- North German armies cannot use more than one battle group of halberdiers or *bidenhänder*

wielders, nor any battle wagons.
- Medieval German City League allied commanders' contingents must conform to the Medieval German City League allies list below, but the troops in the contingent are deducted from the minima and maxima in the main list.
- Only one non-German allied contingent can be used.

Crossbowman

MEDIEVAL GERMAN CITY LEAGUES

Territory Types: Agricultural, Developed, Hilly, Woodland

C-in-C		Inspired Commander/Field Commander/Troop Commander			80/50/35		1	
Sub-commanders		Field Commander			50		0–2	
		Troop Commander			35		0–3	
Troop name		**Troop Type**				**Capabilities**	**Points per base**	**Bases per BG**	**Total bases**
		Type	Armour	Quality	Training	Shooting	Impact			

Troop name		Type	Armour	Quality	Training	Shooting	Impact	Points per base	Bases per BG	Total bases
Core Troops										
Feudal or mercenary men-at-arms		Knights	Heavily Armoured	Superior	Undrilled	–	Lancers, Swordsmen	23	4–6	0–8
Mercenary men-at-arms		Knights	Heavily Armoured	Average	Drilled	–	Lancers, Swordsmen	21	4–6	
Konstaflers		Knights	Heavily Armoured	Average	Undrilled	–	Swordsmen	17	4–6	0–6
Lighter men-at-arms	Only from 1450	Cavalry	Armoured	Average	Undrilled	–	Lancers, Swordsmen	12	4–6	0–6
					Drilled			13		
Mounted crossbowmen		Cavalry	Armoured	Average	Drilled	Crossbow	Swordsmen	14	4–6	0–8	0–8
Mounted handgunners	Only from 1450	Cavalry	Armoured	Average	Drilled	Firearm	Swordsmen	13	4–6	0–4	
Militia spearmen		Heavy Foot	Protected	Average	Drilled	–	Defensive Spearmen	7	6–10	0–48
				Average	Undrilled			6		
				Poor	Drilled			5		
				Poor	Undrilled			4		
Halberdiers		Heavy Foot	Protected	Average	Undrilled	–	Heavy Weapon	7	6–8	0–16
			Protected		Drilled			8		
			Armoured		Undrilled			9		
			Armoured		Drilled			10		
Bidenhänder wielders		Heavy Foot	Protected	Average	Undrilled	–	Heavy Weapon	7	4–8	24–64 / 0–8
			Protected		Drilled			8		
			Armoured		Undrilled			9		
			Armoured		Drilled			10		
Landsknecht 'verlorene haufen'	Only from 1488	Medium or Heavy Foot	Protected	Superior	Drilled	–	Heavy Weapon	10	4–8	
			Armoured					13		
Mercenary or good quality militia spears		Heavy Foot	Armoured	Average	Drilled	–	Defensive Spearmen	9	6–8	6–36
					Undrilled			8		
Pikemen	Only from 1450	Heavy Foot	Protected	Poor	Drilled	–	Pikemen	4	8–12	6–36
Landsknecht pikemen	Only from 1488	Heavy Foot	Protected	Average	Drilled	–	Pikemen	6	8–12	
Militia or mercenary crossbowmen		Medium Foot	Protected	Average	Drilled	Crossbow	–	7	6–8	6–32
			Protected	Average	Undrilled			6		6–32
			Unprotected	Average	Undrilled			5		
			Unprotected	Poor	Undrilled			3		
		Light Foot	Unprotected	Average	Drilled or Undrilled	Crossbow	–	5	6–8	0–8
				Poor				3		
Handgunners	Only from 1375	Light Foot	Protected	Average	Drilled	Firearm	–	5	4–6	0–8
			Unprotected					4		0–12
Landsknecht handgunners	Only from 1488	Light Foot	Protected	Average	Drilled	Firearm	–	5	4–6	0–8

Optional Troops										
Free Canton spearmen	Only north German	Medium Foot	Unprotected	Average	Undrilled	–	Offensive Spearmen	6	6–8	0–24
			Protected					7		
Free Canton javelinmen		Light Foot	Unprotected	Average	Undrilled	Javelin	Light Spears	4	4–6	0–6
			Protected					2		
Free Canton archers		Light Foot	Unprotected	Average	Undrilled	Bow	–	5	4–6	
Hanse marine spearmen		Medium Foot	Protected	Average	Undrilled	–	Light Spear, Swordsmen	6	6–8	0–8
			Armoured					8		
Fußknechte	Only before 1400	Heavy or Medium Foot	Protected	Average	Undrilled	–	Swordsmen	6	6–8	0–12
				Poor				4		
Ill–armed townsfolk		Mob	Unprotected	Poor	Undrilled	–	–	2	10–12	
Light guns	Any date	Light Artillery	–	Average	Undrilled	Light Artillery	–	15	2	0–4
	Only from 1425	Battle Wagons	–	Average	Undrilled	Light Artillery	–	20	2	0–2 / 0–4
Bombards	Only from 1375	Heavy Artillery	–	Average	Undrilled	Heavy Artillery	–	20	2	0–2
War wagons	Only from 1425	Battle Wagons	–	Average	Undrilled	Crossbow	Heavy Weapon	23	2–4	0–8
Landwehren, Letzen or Schanzen		Field Fortifications						3		0–12
Fortified camp								24		0–1

Allies
German allies – Later Medieval German Feudal or Medieval German City League
Low Country allies (Only north German) – Later Low Countries – See Field of Glory Companion 2: *Storm of Arrows*
Swiss allies (Only before 1488) – See Field of Glory Companion 2: *Storm of Arrows*

Special Campaigns										
Swabian Wars (1499)										
Georgschild League men-at-arms		Knights	Heavily Armoured	Superior	Undrilled	–	Lancers, Swordsmen	23	4–6	4–8
Georgschild League lighter men-at-arms		Cavalry	Armoured	Average	Undrilled	–	Lancers, Swordsmen	12	4–6	4–8
Welsche Garde		Knights	Heavily Armoured	Superior	Drilled	–	Lancers, Swordsmen	26	4	0–4 / 0–6
Italian mercenary men-at-arms		Knights	Heavily Armoured	Average	Drilled	–	Lancers, Swordsmen	21	4–6	0–6
Georgschild League mounted handgunners		Cavalry	Armoured	Average	Drilled	Firearm	Swordsmen	13	4–6	0–4
Tiroler Erzknappen		Heavy Foot	Protected	Superior	Undrilled	–	Defensive Spearmen	8	4–6	0–6
Cannot use any allies, *Konstaflers*, nor options available only to north German armies.										

MEDIEVAL GERMAN CITY LEAGUE ALLIES

Allied commander		Field Commander/Troop Commander					40/25	1	
Troop name		**Troop Type**				**Capabilities**	**Points per base**	**Bases per BG**	**Total bases**
		Type	Armour	Quality	Training	Shooting	Impact		
Feudal or mercenary men-at-arms		Knights	Heavily Armoured	Superior	Undrilled	–	Lancers, Swordsmen	23	4	0–4
Mercenary men-at-arms		Knights	Heavily Armoured	Average	Drilled	–	Lancers, Swordsmen	21	4	
Konstaflers		Knights	Heavily Armoured	Average	Undrilled	–	Swordsmen	17	4	
Lighter men-at-arms	Only from 1450	Cavalry	Armoured	Average	Undrilled	–	Lancers, Swordsmen	12	4	0–4
					Drilled			13		
Mounted crossbowmen		Cavalry	Armoured	Average	Drilled	Crossbow	Swordsmen	14	4	
Militia spearmen		Heavy Foot	Protected	Average	Drilled	–	Defensive Spearmen	7	6–10	0–16
				Average	Undrilled			6		
				Poor Average	Drilled			5		
				Poor	Undrilled			4		
Halberdiers		Heavy Foot	Protected	Average	Undrilled	–	Heavy Weapon	7	4–6	0–6
			Protected		Drilled			8		
			Armoured		Undrilled			9		
			Armoured		Drilled			10		
Bidenhänder wielders		Heavy Foot	Protected	Average	Undrilled	–	Heavy Weapon	7	4	8–24
			Protected		Drilled			8		
			Armoured		Undrilled			9		0–4
			Armoured		Drilled			10		
Landsknecht 'verlorene haufen'	Only from 1488	Medium or Heavy Foot	Protected	Superior	Drilled	–	Heavy Weapon	10	4	
			Armoured					13		
Mercenary or good quality militia spears		Heavy Foot	Armoured	Average	Drilled	–	Defensive Spearmen	9	6–8	
					Undrilled			8		
Pikemen	Only from 1450	Heavy Foot	Protected	Poor	Drilled	–	Pikemen	4	8–12	0–12
Landsknecht pikemen	Only from 1488	Heavy Foot	Protected	Average	Drilled	–	Pikemen	6	8–12	
Militia or mercenary crossbowmen		Medium Foot	Protected	Average	Drilled	Crossbow	–	7	4–8	4–8
			Protected	Average	Undrilled			6		
			Unprotected	Average	Undrilled			5		4–10
			Unprotected	Poor	Undrilled			3		
		Light Foot	Unprotected	Average	Drilled or Undrilled	Crossbow	–	5	4	0–4
				Poor				3		
Handgunners	Only from 1375	Light Foot	Protected	Average	Drilled	Firearm	–	5	4–6	0–4
			Unprotected					4		0–4
Landsknecht handgunners	Only from 1488	Light Foot	Protected	Average	Drilled	Firearm	–	5	4–6	0–4
Hanse marine spearmen		Medium Foot	Protected	Average	Undrilled	–	Light Spear, Swordsmen	6	4	0–4
			Armoured					8		
Fußknechte	Only before 1400	Heavy or Medium Foot	Protected	Average	Undrilled	–	Swordsmen	6	4	0–4
			Poor					4		
War wagons	Only from 1425	Battle Wagons	–	Average	Undrilled	Crossbow	Heavy Weapon	23	2	0–2

LATER MEDIEVAL FEUDAL GERMAN

This list covers the Feudal armies of the German princes and other powerful nobles as well as those of various knightly leagues (most of which were short lived, founded only to combat the rising power of the city leagues) from 1340 to 1500. It can be used in themed tournaments based on Field of Glory Companion 2: *Storm of Arrows*. The Later Medieval Feudal German allies list can be used instead of the Later Medieval German list for German allies in a Later Medieval Danish army.

During this time the more powerful nobles were continually competing among themselves. To avoid a strong Emperor intervening, they were careful to elect someone either lacking the resources to impose his will or who would be busy elsewhere – such as Ruprecht I, who was in dire financial straits, or Albrecht II, who was embroiled in the Hussite Wars and the ongoing struggle of Hungary against the Ottomans. This did not prevent the princes from officially lamenting the fact that the Emperors seemingly never took any real interest in German home affairs.

The rising wealth and power of the cities, and especially the city leagues, was seen as a threat by many lesser nobles. Not a few of them made their living from preying on merchants. This could be achieved indirectly by creating

King John of Bohemia

toll stations wherever it pleased them (despite the fact that this was forbidden at least on the *Reichsstreets* and rivers, which saw the majority of the trade). However, the more destitute or depraved scorned any such justification and simply robbed the merchants directly. Where city leagues were established to prevent such actions, the nobles often responded by forming knightly leagues to combat the city leagues. Most of these knightly leagues were short lived, but a few longer lasting ones managed to achieve some sort of agreement with the cities and the more powerful nobles, who also tended to take a dim view of most of these knightly leagues.

TROOP NOTES

Feudal German armies were comparatively conservative in both their organisation and their troop types. Despite the success of the Landsknechts in the late 15th century they made only very limited use of them. This probably stemmed from a certain reluctance to disturb the status quo that had developed between the various German princes, allowing them to wage war on each other directly or via proxy (i.e. lesser nobles sworn to them) without too much damage to the population. Landsknecht armies, by contrast, could (and often did) ravage entire areas for supplies or for loot. Since most wars of the princes were essentially amongst themselves, limiting damage was important to them. Too much damage to the towns and cities, or too many killed civilians (directly or from starvation), and even the victor of a conflict could turn out to be poorer than before. Yet reliance on mercenaries and infantry was increasing even amongst the princes.

German knight and attendants, by Angus McBride. Taken from Men-At-Arms 166: German Medieval Armies 1300–1500.

Whether mercenary men-at-arms were less bold or more disciplined than feudal ones is open to doubt, as they were often nobles themselves.

Fußknechte

Lighter men-at-arms are basically knights who could not afford the full armour panoply of the time, resorting to refurbished older armours and forgoing horse barding. Initially they were deployed in the rear ranks of normal knight formations. Over time they were increasingly moved into separate units to make use of the higher mobility they could achieve. This led to them taking on a different tactical role, acting as the vanguard or rearguard of an army, as out-flankers or to protect flanks. In pitched battles they often dismounted to fight.

Fußknechte were followers armed with a miscellany of weapons, mostly short spears, morningstars, warflails, clubs and swords. We treat this mixture as equivalent to Swordsmen capability.

LATER MEDIEVAL FEUDAL GERMAN STARTER ARMY (AFTER 1450 AD)

Commander-in-Chief	1	Field Commander
Sub-commanders	2	2 x Troop Commander
Feudal or mercenary men-at-arms	2 BGs	Each comprising 4 bases of men-at-arms: Superior, Heavily Armoured, Undrilled Knights – Lancers, Swordsmen
Lighter men-at-arms	2 BGs	Each comprising 4 bases of lighter men-at-arms: Average, Armoured, Undrilled Cavalry – Lancers, Swordsmen
Mercenary or good quality militia spearmen	1 BG	8 bases of mercenary or good quality militia spearmen: Average, Armoured, Drilled Heavy Foot – Defensive Spearmen
Feudal or militia spearmen	1 BG	8 bases of feudal or militia spearmen: Average, Protected, Undrilled Heavy Foot – Defensive Spearmen
Militia or mercenary crossbowmen	1 BG	8 bases of militia or mercenary crossbowmen: Average, Protected, Drilled Medium Foot – Crossbow
Handgunners	1 BG	6 bases of handgunners: Average, Unprotected, Drilled Light Foot – Firearm
Camp	1	Unfortified camp
Total	8 BGs	Camp, 16 mounted bases, 30 foot bases, 3 commanders

BUILDING A CUSTOMISED LIST USING OUR ARMY POINTS

Choose an army based on the maxima and minima in the list below. The following special instructions apply to this army:

- Commanders should be depicted as knights.
- Feudal or mercenary men-at-arms can always dismount as Superior or Average (as mounted type), Heavily Armoured, Undrilled or Drilled (as mounted type), Heavy Foot – Heavy Weapon.
- Lighter Men-at-Arms can always dismount as Average, Heavily Armoured, Undrilled or Drilled (as mounted type), Heavy Foot – Heavy Weapon.
- Fußknechte can be graded as Heavy Foot or Medium Foot but all must be graded the same.
- Later Medieval Feudal German allied commanders' contingents must conform to the Later Medieval Feudal German allies list below, but the troops in the contingent are deducted from the minima and maxima in the main list.
- The minimum marked * is reduced to 4 from 1450.
- Swiss allies cannot be used with Landsknechts or Danish allies.

LATER MEDIEVAL FEUDAL GERMAN

Territory Types: Agricultural, Developed, Hilly, Woodland

C-in-C		Inspired Commander/Field Commander/Troop Commander					80/50/35	1	
Sub-commanders		Field Commander					50	0–2	
		Troop Commander					35	0–3	

Troop name		Troop Type				Capabilities		Points per base	Bases per BG	Total bases
		Type	Armour	Quality	Training	Shooting	Impact			
Core Troops										
Feudal or mercenary men-at-arms		Knights	Heavily Armoured	Superior	Undrilled	–	Lancers, Swordsmen	23	4–6	4–16	*8–16
Mercenary men-at-arms		Knights	Heavily Armoured	Average	Drilled	–	Lancers, Swordsmen	21	4–6	0–8
Lighter men-at-arms	Only from 1450	Cavalry	Armoured	Average	Undrilled	–	Lancers, Swordsmen	12	4–6	4–16
					Drilled			13		
Mounted crossbowmen		Cavalry	Armoured	Average	Drilled	Crossbow	Swordsmen	14	4–6	0–8
Mounted handgunners	Only from 1480	Cavalry	Armoured	Average	Drilled	Firearm	Swordsmen	13	4–6	0–4
Feudal or militia spearmen		Heavy Foot	Protected	Average	Drilled	–	Defensive Spearmen	7	6–10	6–48
				Average	Undrilled			6		
				Poor	Drilled			5		
				Poor	Undrilled			4		
Halberdiers		Heavy Foot	Protected	Average	Undrilled	–	Heavy Weapon	7	4–8	0–8	12–50
			Protected		Drilled			8		
			Armoured		Undrilled			9		
			Armoured		Drilled			10		
Mercenary or good quality militia spearmen		Heavy Foot	Armoured	Average	Drilled	–	Defensive Spearmen	9	6–8	6–36
					Undrilled			8		
Landsknecht pikemen	Only from 1490	Heavy Foot	Protected	Average	Drilled	–	Pikemen	6	8–12	0–16
Militia or mercenary crossbowmen		Medium Foot	Protected	Average	Drilled	Crossbow	–	7	6–8	6–24	6–24
			Protected	Average	Undrilled			6		
			Unprotected	Average	Undrilled			5		
			Unprotected	Poor	Undrilled			3		
		Light Foot	Unprotected	Average	Drilled or Undrilled	Crossbow	–	5	6–8	0–8
				Poor				3		
Handgunners	Only from 1400	Light Foot	Protected	Average	Drilled	Firearm	–	5	4–6	0–8
			Unprotected					4		
Optional Troops										
Fußknechte	Only before 1400	Heavy or Medium Foot	Protected	Average	Undrilled	–	Swordsmen	6	6–8	0–12
				Poor				4		
Ill-armed townsfolk		Mob	Unprotected	Poor	Undrilled	–	–	2	10–12	
Light guns	Any date	Light Artillery	–	Average	Undrilled	Light Artillery	–	15	2	0–2
Bombards	Only from 1375	Heavy Artillery	–	Average	Undrilled	Heavy Artillery	–	20	2	0–2
Landwehren, Letzen or Schanzen		Field Fortifications						3		0–12
Fortified camp								24		0–1
Allies										
Danish allies – Later Medieval Danish										
German allies – Later Medieval German Feudal or Medieval German City League										
Swiss allies – See Field of Glory Companion 2: Storm of Arrows										

LATER MEDIEVAL FEUDAL GERMAN ALLIES

Allied commander		Field Commander/ Troop Commander					40/25		1	
Troop name		Troop Type				Capabilities		Points per base	Bases per BG	Total bases
		Type	Armour	Quality	Training	Shooting	Impact			
Feudal or mercenary men-at-arms		Knights	Heavily Armoured	Superior	Undrilled	–	Lancers, Swordsmen	23	4–6	4–8
Mercenary men-at-arms		Knights	Heavily Armoured	Average	Drilled	–	Lancers, Swordsmen	21	4–6	0–4
Lighter men-at-arms	Only from 1450	Cavalry	Armoured	Average	Undrilled	–	Lancers, Swordsmen	12	4–6	4–8
					Drilled			13		
Mounted crossbowmen		Cavalry	Armoured	Average	Drilled	Crossbow	Swordsmen	14	4	0–4
Mounted handgunners	Only from 1480	Cavalry	Armoured	Average	Drilled	Firearm	Swordsmen	13	4	0–4
Feudal or Milita spearmen		Heavy Foot	Protected	Average	Drilled	–	Defensive Spearmen	7	6–10	0–20
				Average	Undrilled			6		
				Poor	Drilled			5		
				Poor	Undrilled			4		
Halberdiers		Heavy Foot	Protected	Average	Undrilled	–	Heavy Weapon	7	4	0–4
			Protected		Drilled			8		
			Armoured		Undrilled			9		
			Armoured		Drilled			10		
Mercenary or good quality militia spears		Heavy Foot	Armoured	Average	Drilled	–	Defensive Spearmen	9	6–8	0–16
					Undrilled			8		
Militia or mercenary crossbowmen		Medium Foot	Protected	Average	Drilled	Crossbow	–	7	6–8	0–12
			Protected	Average	Undrilled			6		
			Unprotected	Average	Undrilled			5		
			Unprotected	Poor	Undrilled			3		
Handgunners	Only from 1400	Light Foot	Protected	Average	Drilled	Firearm	–	5	4	0–4
			Unprotected					4		
Fußknechte	Only before 1400	Heavy or Medium Foot	Protected	Average	Undrilled	–	Swordsmen	6	6	0–6
				Poor				4		

Total bases range **4–8** for the first two Knights rows, **6–24** for the Heavy Foot spearmen/halberdiers grouping.

LATER MEDIEVAL DANISH ALLIES

Allied commander		Field Commander/ Troop Commander					40/25		1	
Troop name		Troop Type				Capabilities		Points per base	Bases per BG	Total bases
		Type	Armour	Quality	Training	Shooting	Close Combat			
Feudal men-at-arms		Knights	Heavily Armoured	Superior	Undrilled	–	Lancers, Swordsmen	23	4–6	4–8
				Average				18		
Select levy		Heavy Foot	Armoured	Average	Drilled	–	Heavy Weapon	10	1/2 or all	6–8
		Medium Foot	Armoured	Average	Drilled	Crossbow	Swordsmen	10	1/2 or none	6–12
		Heavy Foot	Armoured	Average	Undrilled	–	Heavy Weapon	9	1/2 or all	6–8
		Medium Foot	Armoured	Average	Undrilled	Crossbow	Swordsmen	9	1/2 or none	
General levy		Heavy Foot	Protected	Poor	Undrilled	–	Defensive spearmen	4	1/2, 2/3 or all	6–9
		Light Foot	Unprotected	Poor	Undrilled	Crossbow		3	1/2, 1/3 or none	0–27
						Bow		3		

LATER MEDIEVAL FRISIAN OR DITHMARSCHEN

This list covers the armies of the "autonomous peasant republics", also known as the Free Cantons, from 1340 until the defeat of the last significant army they ever fielded in 1500. It can be used in themed tournaments based on Field of Glory Companion 2: *Storm of Arrows*.

While formally belonging to this powerful noble or that city, the Free Cantons were effectively independent. Frisia was the largest.

Frisia, especially, was by no means a unified area. Internal strife was common, but rarely took the form of field battles – lightning raids being much more common. Whenever outside powers tried to take advantage, however, they usually found the Free Cantoners united, with all internal squabbles suspended.

All attempts to bring them to heel failed, often at great cost to the would-be conquerors. In large part this was due to the inaccessible terrain. It also helped that most of the nominal overlords were not that interested in subjugating these people, having identified the cost of doing so and the comparatively low value of what they stood to gain.

Now and then parts of the Free Cantons, especially Frisia with its prosperous cities, were formally subjugated. They usually soon revolted, however, renouncing all obligations to their so-called overlords. At times they invited outside powers to protect them, but never for long.

In the case of Frisia, the most dangerous opponents were the counts of Holland, who at one time had pacified almost all of Frisia, or so they thought. As always, however, the Frisians soon revolted. They defeated major invasions by Holland in 1345 and 1396. Frisia was conquered in 1498 by the Habsburgs.

Dithmarschen formally belonged to the Arch-Bishop of Bremen, however only the Danish managed to conquer them once, for a short while, before the start of this period. Other attempts to conquer them, like the attacks by Holstein armies in 1319 and 1404, met with failure. In 1500 Dithmarschen defeated a combined Danish–Holstein army at Hemmingstedt, which bought them another 59 years of relative independence. After losing that battle, Holstein started to use more subtle means to gradually draw many of the wealthier and more influential families over to its side. This policy was sufficiently successful that in 1559, when Dithmarschen was finally conquered, resistance was weak and short-lived.

TROOP NOTES

Due to the terrain these armies fought in and their defensive strategies their knights seem to have fought mainly dismounted.

Crossbowmen

The "fortifications" used were sometimes palisades or earth walls, but in most cases consisted of drainage channels.

The pole spear used by the Free Cantoners was held in both hands, precluding the use of a shield. It had a disk on the butt end (up to 20cm in diameter) to prevent it sinking into the mud

Handgunners

when it was used as a 'vaulting pole' to quickly and safely jump over drainage channels, small bogs or other treacherous terrain features. This allowed the users unmatched mobility in marshy terrain. There is also mention of long swords, axes and similar weapons. We subsume these into the spearmen, however, as their numbers were probably not great, nor does it seem that they were used in separate units.

It is unclear whether the Landsknechts hired during the last weeks of 1499, in anticipation of attack from the dukes of Holstein, ever saw battle. Shortly before the attack materialized, at least some of them either left or were disbanded again, for unknown reasons. It is fairly certain that no Landsknechts fought in the Dithmarschen army at Hemmingstedt.

DITHMARSCHEN STARTER ARMY (AFTER 1420)		
Commander-in-Chief	1	Troop Commander
Sub-commanders	2	2 x Troop Commander
Free Canton knights	1 BG	4 bases of Free Canton knights: Superior, Heavily Armoured, Undrilled Knights – Lancers, Swordsmen
Pole spearmen	5 BGs	Each comprising 8 bases of pole spearmen: Average, Protected, Undrilled Medium Foot – Offensive Spearmen
Crossbowmen	1 BG	8 bases of crossbowmen: Average, Protected, Undrilled Medium Foot – Crossbow
Skirmishing javelinmen	1 BG	8 bases of skirmishing javelinmen: Average, Unprotected, Undrilled Light Foot – Javelins, Light Spear
Handgunners	1 BG	4 bases of handgunners: Average, Unprotected, Undrilled Light Foot – Firearm
Field Fortifications	9	9 bases frontage of field fortifications
Camp	1	Unfortified camp
Total	9 BGs	Camp, 4 mounted bases, 60 foot bases, 3 commanders, 8 field fortifications

BUILDING A CUSTOMISED LIST USING OUR ARMY POINTS

Choose an army based on the maxima and minima in the list below. The following special instructions apply to this army:

- Commanders should be depicted as pole spearmen or knights.
- Knights can always dismount as Superior, Heavily Armoured, Undrilled Heavy Foot – Heavy Weapon.
- Frisian or Dithmarschen allied commanders'

contingents must conform to the Later Medieval Frisian or Dithmarschen allies list below, but the troops in the contingent are deducted from the minima and maxima in the main list.

- Only one allied contingent can be used.

LATER MEDIEVAL FRISIAN OR DITHMARSCHEN

Territory Types: Agricultural, Developed

C-in-C	Inspired Commander/Field Commander/Troop Commander					80/50/35	1	
Sub-commanders	Field Commander					50	0–2	
	Troop Commander					35	0–3	
Frisian or Dithmarschen allied commanders	Field Commander/Troop Commander					40/25	0–2	

Troop name	Troop Type				Capabilities		Points per base	Bases per BG	Total bases
	Type	Armour	Quality	Training	Shooting	Impact			
Core Troops									
Free Canton knights	Knights	Heavily Armoured	Superior	Undrilled	–	Lancers Swordsmen	23	4	0–4
	Heavy Foot	Heavily Armoured	Superior	Undrilled	–	Heavy Weapon	14	4	
Pole spearmen	Medium Foot	Protected	Average	Undrilled	–	Offensive Spearmen	7	6–10	24–130
		Unprotected					6		
Crossbowmen	Medium Foot	Protected	Average	Undrilled	Crossbow	–	6	6–8	0–12 / 6–12
		Unprotected					5		
	Light Foot	Unprotected	Average	Undrilled	Crossbow	–	5	6–8	0–8
Archers	Medium Foot	Protected	Average	Undrilled	Bow	–	6	6–8	0–8
		Unprotected					5		
	Light Foot	Unprotected	Average	Undrilled	Bow	–	5	6–8	
Skirmishing javelinmen	Light Foot	Unprotected	Average	Undrilled	Javelins	Light Spear	4	6–8	6–24
Field fortifications	Field Fortifications						3		8–48
Optional Troops									
Handgunners	Only from 1420	Light Foot	Unprotected	Average	Undrilled	Firearm	–	4	4–6	0–8
			Protected					5		
Fortified camp								24	0–1
Allies									
Danish allies – Later Medieval Danish									
German allies – Medieval German City League (only Dithmarschen) or Later Medieval German Feudal									
Special Campaigns Only Dithmarschen in 1500									
Only Dithmarschen in 1500									
Landsknecht pikemen	Heavy Foot	Protected	Average	Drilled	–	Pikemen	6	8–12	16–24
Landsknecht handgunners	Light Foot	Protected	Average	Drilled	Firearm	–	5	4–8	6–8
Landsknecht crossbowmen	Medium Foot	Protected	Average	Drilled	Crossbow	–	7	4–6	0–6
No allies are permitted.									

LATER MEDIEVAL FRISIAN OR DITHMARSCHEN ALLIES

Allied commander		Field Commander/Troop Commander					40/25		1
Troop name		Troop Type				Capabilities		Points per base	Bases per BG	Total bases
	Type	Armour	Quality	Training	Shooting	Impact			
Pole spearmen	Medium Foot	Protected	Average	Undrilled	–	Offensive Spearmen	7	6–10	8–24
		Unprotected					6		
Crossbowmen	Medium Foot	Protected	Average	Undrilled	Crossbow	–	6	6–8	0–4
		Unprotected					5		
	Light Foot	Unprotected	Average	Undrilled	Crossbow	–	5	6–8	
Archers	Medium Foot	Protected	Average	Undrilled	Bow	–	6	6–8	
		Unprotected					5		
	Light Foot	Unprotected	Average	Undrilled	Bow	–	5	6–8	
Skirmishing javelinmen	Light Foot	Unprotected	Average	Undrilled	Javelins	Light Spear	4	6–8	0–8

APPENDIX 1 – USING THE LISTS

To give balanced games, armies can be selected using the points system. The more effective the troops, the more each base costs in points. The maximum points for an army will usually be set at between 600 and 800 points for a singles game for 2 to 4 hours play. We recommend 800 points for 15mm singles tournament games (650 points for 25mm) and 1000 points for 15mm doubles games.

Bombard deployed for action

The army lists specify which troops can be used in a particular army. No other troops can be used. The number of bases of each type in the army must conform to the specified minima and maxima. Troops that have restrictions on when they can be used cannot be used with troops with a conflicting restriction. For example, troops that can only be used "before 340" cannot be used with troops that can only be used "from 340". All special instructions applying to an army list must be adhered to. They also apply to allied contingents supplied by the army.

All armies must have a C-in-C and at least one other commander. No army can have more than 4 commanders in total, including C-in-C, sub-commanders and allied commanders.

All armies must have a supply camp. This is free unless fortified. A fortified camp can only be used if specified in the army list. Field fortifications and portable defences can only be used if specified in the army list.

Allied contingents can only be used if specified in the army list. Most allied contingents have their own allied contingent list, to which they must conform unless the main army's list specifies otherwise.

BATTLE GROUPS

All troops are organized into battle groups. Commanders, supply camps and field fortifications are not troops and are not assigned to battle groups. Portable defences are not troops, but are assigned to specific battle groups.

Battle groups must obey the following restrictions:

- The number of bases in a battle group must correspond to the range specified in the army list.
- Each battle group must initially comprise an even number of bases. The only exception to this rule is that battle groups whose army list specifies them as 2/3 of one type and 1/3 of another, can comprise 9 bases if this is within the battle group size range specified by the list.

- A battle group can only include troops from one line in a list, unless the list specifies a mixed formation by specifying fractions of the battle group to be of types from two lines. e.g. 2/3 spearmen, 1/3 archers.
- All troops in a battle group must be of the same quality and training. When a choice of quality or training is given in a list, this allows battle groups to differ from each other. It does not permit variety within a battle group.
- Unless specifically stated otherwise in an army list, all troops in a battle group must be of the same armour class. When a choice of armour class is given in a list, this allows battle groups to differ from each other. It does not permit variety within a battle group.

EXAMPLE LIST

Here is a section of an actual army list, which will help us to explain the basics and some special features. The list specifies the following items for each historical type included in the army:

- Troop Type - comprising Type, Armour, Quality and Training.
- Capabilities – comprising Shooting and Close Combat capabilities.
- Points cost per base.
- Minimum and maximum number of bases in each battle group.
- Minimum and maximum number of bases in the army.

Troop name	Troop Type				Capabilities		Points per base	Bases per BG	Total bases
	Type	Armour	Quality	Training	Shooting	Close Combat			
City cavalry	Cavalry	Armoured	Superior	Undrilled	–	Lancers, Swordsmen	16	4–6	0–6
		Armoured	Average				12		
		Protected	Superior				12		
		Protected	Average				9		
Foot warriors	Heavy Foot	Protected	Average	Undrilled	–	Light Spear, Swordsmen	6	2/3 or all	24–120
Supporting archers	Light Foot	Unprotected	Average	Undrilled	Bow	–	5	1/3 or 0	0–24
Separately deployed archers	Medium Foot	Protected	Average	Undrilled	Bow	–	6	6–8	0–24
	Light Foot	Unprotected	Average	Undrilled	Bow	–	5	6–8	0–12
Bedouin cavalry	Light Horse	Unprotected	Average	Undrilled	–	Lancers, Swordsmen	8	4–6	0–8
	Cavalry	Unprotected	Average	Undrilled	–	Lancers, Swordsmen	8	4–6	
		Protected					9		

SPECIAL FEATURES

- City cavalry can be organized in a battle group of 4 or 6 bases. They can be graded as Armoured Superior, Armoured Average, Protected Superior or Protected Average. All of the bases in the battle group must be graded the same. The list gives the points cost for each grading. The total number of bases of city cavalry in the army cannot exceed 6.
- Each foot warrior battle group can either be all foot warrior Heavy Foot or 2/3 foot warrior Heavy Foot, 1/3 supporting Light Foot archers. It is permitted for some battle groups to be all Heavy Foot and some to be mixed. If all Heavy Foot, each battle group must be of 8 bases. If mixed, each battle group must be of 9 bases. The minimum total number of foot warrior Heavy Foot bases in the army is 24, and the maximum is 120. The maximum total number of supporting archer Light Foot bases in the army is 24.
- Separately deployed archers can be fielded as Medium Foot or Light Foot. All the bases in a battle group must be classified the same, but different battle groups can be different. Each battle group can be of 6 or 8 bases. The maximum total number of bases of separately deployed archers in the army is 12. The maximum combined total number of bases of supporting and separately deployed archers in the army is 24.
- Bedouin cavalry can be fielded as Unprotected Light Horse or as Unprotected or Protected Cavalry. All the bases in a battle group must be classified the same, but different battle groups can be different. Each battle group can be of 4 or 6 bases. The maximum total number of bases of Bedouin cavalry in the army is 8.

Etruscan 2nd class Infantrymen

APPENDIX 2 – THEMED TOURNAMENTS

The following lists from this book can be used in the tournament themes specified below:

SEVEN HILLS

Early Republican Roman
Etruscan League
Italian Hill Tribes
Latin
Samnite
Campanian
Apulian, Lucanian or Bruttian

And also the following list from Field of Glory Companion 1: *Rise of Rome*
Gallic

RISE OF ROME

Early Republican Roman
Etruscan League
Italian Hill Tribes
Latin

Samnite
Campanian
Apulian, Lucanian or Bruttian

STORM OF ARROWS

Medieval German City Leagues
Later Medieval Feudal German
Later Medieval Frisian or Dithmarschen

LEGIONS TRIUMPHANT

Pre-Islamic Arabian
Later Pre-Islamic Bedouin
Beja, Nile valley Blemmye or Early Nobatae

DECLINE AND FALL

Pre-Islamic Arabian
Later Pre-Islamic Bedouin
Axumite
Beja, Nile valley Blemmye or Early Nobatae

SWIFTER THAN EAGLES

Early Nomad
Early Highland Raiders
Early Elamite
Amorite Kingdoms

EMPIRES OF THE DRAGON

Vietnamese

Etruscan Chariot

INDEX